SpringerBriefs in Computer Science

T0213862

More information about this series at http://www.springer.com/series/10028

Ran He • Baogang Hu • Xiaotong Yuan
Liang Wang

Robust Recognition via Information Theoretic Learning

Springer

Ran He
National Laboratory
  of Pattern Recognition
Institute of Automation
  Chinese Academy of Sciences
Beijing, China

Xiaotong Yuan
School of Information
  and Control
Nanjing University of Information
  Science and Technology
Nanjing, China

Baogang Hu
National Laboratory
  of Pattern Recognition
Institute of Automation
  Chinese Academy of Sciences
Beijing, China

Liang Wang
National Laboratory
  of Pattern Recognition
Institute of Automation
  Chinese Academy of Sciences
Beijing, China

ISSN 2191-5768   ISSN 2191-5776 (electronic)
ISBN 978-3-319-07415-3   ISBN 978-3-319-07416-0 (eBook)
DOI 10.1007/978-3-319-07416-0
Springer Cham Heidelberg New York Dordrecht London

Library of Congress Control Number: 2014944531

Printed on acid-free paper

Springer is part of Springer Science+Business Media (www.springer.com)

To my parents Guocai He and Shuhua Wang,
my elder cousin Jie He,
and my wife Linlin Chi

— Ran He

To my parents Zhaosen Hu and Huayun Deng
and my wife Wenzheng Zhang

— Baogang Hu

Acknowledgements

The completion of this book owes to not only the work of the authors but also many more persons and groups. First and foremost, we would like to thank Dr. Tieniu Tan for always trusting and supporting us. Without his help and understanding, we could not finish this book. We also thank Dr. Jose C. Principe for his 20 years' research efforts in information theoretic learning, which makes this book theoretically solid. We thank our friends, especially Dr. Wei-Shi Zheng, Dr. Zhennan Sun, and Dr. Kaiqi Huang, who showed us the ropes in machine learning and computer vision. Special thanks to Mrs. Hegde Ritya, Dr. Xiang-Wei Kong, Dr. Jing Dong, and Miss. Jessica Y. Zhang for helping us revise this book. Second, we want to give thanks to the assistance provided by Courtney Clark and the publication team at SpringerBriefs. We are very thankful to all the members of CRIPAC (www.cripac.ia.ac.cn) and NLPR (www.nlpr.ia.ac.cn) for their help and hard work. And many thanks to the administrative and support staff (Ling Di, Lei Li, Lixia Ma, Wei Zhao, and Guozhen Lian) who makes living and research easier.

Research efforts summarized in this book were supported by the National Basic Research Program of China (Grant No. 2012CB316300), National Natural Science Foundation of China (Grant No. 61103155, 61135002, 61075051, 61175003), and Nanjing University of Information Science and Technology Faculty Startup (Grant No. S8113029001).

Contents

Acronyms

CESR	Correntropy-based sparse representation
CIM	Correntropy induced metric
CS	Compressed sensing
EM	Expectation maximization
FN	False negative
FP	False positive
GMM	Gaussian mixture model
HQ	Half quadratic
KKT	Karush–Kuhn–Tucker
LDA	Linear discriminant analysis
LPP	Locality preserving projections
MaxEnt	Maximum entropy
MCC	Maximum correntropy criterion
mELE	Minimum entropy linear embedding
MSE	Mean square error
NFL	Nearest feature line
NI	Normalized information
NSR	Nonnegative sparse representation
ICA	Independent component analysis
IRLS	Iteratively reweighted least squares
IP	Information potential
ITL	Information theoretic learning
PCA	Principal component analysis
PDF	Probability density function
RN	Reject negative
RP	Reject positive
SRC	Sparse representation classification
SVD	Singular value decomposition
TN	True negative
TP	True positive
TSR	Two-stage sparse representation

Chapter 1
Introduction

Robust data classification or representation is a fundamental task and has a long history in computer vision. The algorithmic robustness, which is derived from the statistical definition of a breakdown point [49,106], is the ability of an algorithm that tolerates a large amount of outliers. Therefore, a robust method should be effective enough to reject outliers in images and perform classification only on uncorrupted pixels. In the past decades, many works for subspace learning [37,91] and sparse signal representation [101,154] have been developed to obtain more robust image-based object recognition. Despite significant improvement, performing robust classification is still challenging due to the nature of unpredictable outliers in an image. Outliers may occupy any parts of an image and have arbitrarily large values in magnitude [155].

Recently, information theoretic learning (ITL) [126,158] has shown its superiority in robust learning and classification. In [59,61,127,165], Renyi's entropy [32] and correntropy [135] are used as cost functions to learn robust subspaces under supervised and unsupervised learning. Liu et al. [99] proves that the correntropy is a robust function (in the sense of Welsch) for linear and nonlinear regression. In [32,122,158,165], the connection between entropy and robust functions has been discussed. The correntropy MACE filter is a detector for automatic target detection and recognition (ATR) [83] and can cope with random subspace projections. In [145,163], feature extraction is achieved by directly maximizing the quadratic mutual information between class label and features. In addition, ITL has been widely used in similarity measure [97,99], mean shift [128], clustering [81, 140, 148, 166], feature selection and extraction [64, 110, 120, 145], metric learning [36], semi-supervised learning [66, 114, 115], information hiding [108], random processes [125], compressed sensing [136], subspace segmentation [170,171], low-rank matrix recovery [62,63], nonnegative matrix factorization [45], etc. Numerical results on these real-world learning tasks have demonstrated that the methods based on information theoretic measures can make algorithms robust to noise.

© The Author(s) 2014
R. He et al., *Robust Recognition via Information Theoretic Learning*,
SpringerBriefs in Computer Science, DOI 10.1007/978-3-319-07416-0_1

Since ITL involves a large scope in robust learning, we could not include all that we wished, and restrict the topics of this monograph only to Renyi's quadratic entropy and its derived correntropy. We beg the forgiveness of researchers whose contributions have not been duly cited. In the following chapters of this monograph, we will present an overview of the theories and methods of information theoretic measures and examine several robust classification or representation applications based on these theories. We will also explore the use of entropy to model robust sparse representation problems and the relationship between the robustness of M-estimators and parameter settings.

1.1 Outline

We begin this monograph with a brief introduction on the theories related to ITL in Chap. 2. In particular, we present some fundamental premises of ITL: M-estimation and half-quadratic minimization. M-estimation provides a theoretic tool to analyze robustness, and half-quadratic minimization simplifies the optimization of information theoretic loss functions.

In Chap. 3, we describe information theoretic measures for data understanding and abstaining classifications. In particular, we present the fundamental theories of Renyi's quadratic entropy and its applications in robust component analysis. We also discuss how to select information theoretic measures to evaluate the overall quality of classifications. A reject option is considered in classifications which provides an alternative means of achieving robust recognition.

In Chap. 4, we describe the fundamental theories and properties of correntropy and discuss some applications of linear regression in object classification. We show how correntropy can be used to improve the robustness of linear regression and develop robust algorithms for classification. Finally, we discuss the stability of different linear regression methods.

In Chap. 5, we discuss the use of correntropy to improve the robustness of sparse representation. We first resort to half-quadratic minimization to solve sparse signal recovery problems. Then we show a robust sparse representation framework to unify error correction and error detection based robust sparse representation methods. Numerical results on different types of errors are also given to validate the robustness of correntropy.

In Chap. 6, we present an overview of some recent advances in nonnegative sparse representation. In particular, we introduce an ℓ_1 regularized nonnegative sparse coding algorithm and an efficient nonnegative sparse coding algorithm to learn a nonnegative sparse representation. Then we show how to use correntropy to learn a robust and nonnegative sparse representation. Finally, based on the divide and conquer strategy, we present a two-stage framework for large-scale sparse representation problems.

Chapter 2
M-Estimators and Half-Quadratic Minimization

In robust statistics, there are several types of robust estimators, including M-estimator (maximum likelihood type estimator), L-estimator (linear combinations of order statistics), R-estimator (estimator based on rank transformation) [77], RM estimator (repeated median) [141], and LMS estimator (estimator using the least median of squares) [133]. When information theoretic learning is applied to robust statistics, the Gaussian kernel in entropy plays a role of Welsch M-estimator and can be efficiently optimized by half-quadratic minimization. Hence, in this chapter, we introduce some basic concepts of M-estimation and half-quadratic minimization.

2.1 M-Estimation

M-estimators are defined as the minima of summation of functions of a dataset. The statistical procedure of evaluating an M-estimator is called M-estimation, which is defined as a generalized maximum-likelihood method for the following cost function [99, 172]:

$$\min_{\theta} \sum_j \phi(e_j|\theta), \qquad (2.1)$$

where $\phi(.)$ is differentiable and satisfies four conditions (p. 5291, [99]):

$$\phi(t) \geq 0;$$

$$\phi(0) \geq 0;$$

$$\phi(t) = \phi(-t);$$

$$\phi(t) \geq \phi(\bar{t}) \text{ for } |t| > |\bar{t}|$$

© The Author(s) 2014
R. He et al., *Robust Recognition via Information Theoretic Learning*,
SpringerBriefs in Computer Science, DOI 10.1007/978-3-319-07416-0_2

Table 2.1 A few commonly used M-estimators ($\phi(.)$) and their corresponding weighting functions ($w(.)$). c is a constant [172]

Type	$\phi(t)$	$w(t)$
ℓ_1	$|t|$	$1/|t|$
ℓ_1-ℓ_2	$2(\sqrt{1+t^2/2}-1)$	$1/\sqrt{1+t^2/2}$
ℓ_p	$|t|^c/c$	$|t|^{c-2}$
Fair	$c^2(|t|/c - log(1+|t|/c))$	$1/(1+|t|/c)$
Huber $\begin{cases} \text{if}|t| \leq c \\ \text{if}|t| > c \end{cases}$	$\begin{cases} t^2/2 \\ c(|t|-c/2) \end{cases}$	$\begin{cases} 1 \\ c/|t| \end{cases}$
Cauchy	$(c^2/2)log(1+(t/c)^2)$	$1/(1+(t/c)^2)$
Geman-McClure	$t^2/(2(1+t^2))$	$1/(1+t^2)^2$
Welsch	$(c^2/2)(1-exp(t/c)^2)$	$exp((t/c)^2)$
Tukey $\begin{cases} \text{if}|t| \leq c \\ \text{if}|t| > c \end{cases}$	$\begin{cases} \frac{c^2}{6}(1-(1-(t/c)^2))^3 \\ c^2/6 \end{cases}$	$\begin{cases} (1-(t/c)^2)^2 \\ 0 \end{cases}$

and θ is a set of adjustable parameters and e_j is an error produced by a learning system [99]. An M-estimator is often solved by the following iteratively reweighted way:

$$\min_{\theta} \sum_j w(e_j^t)(e_j^2|\theta), \tag{2.2}$$

where $w(.)$ is a weighting function with respect to $\phi(.)$. The weight $w(e_j^t)$ should be recomputed after each iteration in order to be used in the next iteration. Table 2.1 shows nine M-estimators ($\phi(.)$) and their corresponding weighting functions ($w(.)$).

2.2 Half-Quadratic Minimization

Half-quadratic (HQ) minimization was pioneered in [54, 55] for reconstructing images and signals. Then Idier [80] further studied HQ minimization for image restoration. Champagnat and Idier [21] made a connection between HQ minimization and expectation maximization (EM). And a systematic analysis of the global and local convergence of HQ was given in [3, 112]. Recently, HQ minimization and its minimization functions have been widely used in machine learning and computer vision, such as mean-shift [166], image registration and synthesis [71], and robust feature extraction [165]. It is a general optimization method for convex or non-convex minimization based on conjugate function theory.

Given a differentiable function $f(v) : \mathbb{R}^d \to \mathbb{R}$, the conjugate $f^*(p) : \mathbb{R}^d \to \mathbb{R}$ of the function f is defined as [13]

$$f^*(p) = \max_{v \in dom f}(p^T v - f(v)). \tag{2.3}$$

Fig. 2.1 A differentiable
function $f(v) : \mathbb{R} \to \mathbb{R}$ and its
conjugate function $f^*(p)$
with a value p [13]. As shown
by the *dashed line*, the
conjugate function $f^*(p)$ is
the maximum gap between
the linear function vp and
$f(v)$, which occurs at a point
v where $f'(v) = p$ [13]

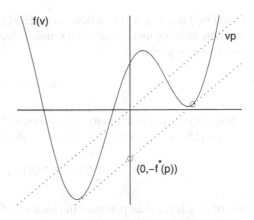

The domain of $f^*(p)$ is bounded above on **dom**f [13]. Since $f^*(p)$ is the point-wise
supremum of a family of convex functions of p, it is a convex function [13]. If $f(v)$
is convex and closed, the conjugate of its conjugate function is itself, i.e., $f^{**} = f$
[13]. Figure 2.1 gives an illustration of a conjugate function.

Based on conjugate function theory, a loss function in image restoration and
signal recovery can be defined as [9, 22, 30]

$$f(v) = \min_p \{Q(v, p) + \varphi(p)\}, \qquad (2.4)$$

where $f(.)$ is a potential loss function (such as M-estimators), v is a set of adjustable
parameters of a linear system, p is an auxiliary variable in HQ optimization, $Q(v, p)$
is a quadratic function ($Q(v, p) \doteq \sum_j p_j v_j^2$ for $p \in \mathbb{R}^d_+$ and $v \in \mathbb{R}^d$, or $Q(v, p) \doteq$
$||v - p||_2^2$ for $p \in \mathbb{R}^d$ and $v \in \mathbb{R}^d$), and $\varphi(.)$ is the dual potential function of $f(.)$.[1]

In the two-step iterative shrinkage/thresholding algorithms [161], the minimization function of (2.4) is also known as proximal mapping [9, 30]; in half-quadratic
methods, the function $Q(v, p) + \varphi(p)$ is called the resultant (augmented) cost-
function of $f(v)$, and can be optimized by a two-step alternating minimization
way [22].

2.2.1 Iterative Minimization

Let $\phi_v(.)$ be a function on a vector $v \in \mathbb{R}^d$ that is defined as

$$\phi_v(v) \doteq \sum_{j=1}^d \phi(v_j), \qquad (2.5)$$

---

[1]Note that for different types of $Q(v, p)$, the dual potential functions $\varphi(.)$ may be different.

where $\phi(.)$ is a potential loss function in HQ [112,165] and v_j is the jth entry of v. In machine learning and compressed sensing, one often aims to compute the following minimization problem:

$$\min_v \phi_v(v) + J(v), \tag{2.6}$$

where $J(v)$ is a convex penalty function on v. According to half-quadratic minimization [54,55], we know that for a fixed v_j, the following equation holds:

$$\phi(v_j) = \min_{p_j} Q(v_j, p_j) + \varphi(p_j), \tag{2.7}$$

where $\varphi(.)$ is the dual potential function of $\phi(.)$, and $Q(v_j, p_j)$ is the half-quadratic function which can be modeled in the additive or the multiplicative form as shown in Sect. 2.2.2. Let $Q_v(v, p) \doteq \sum_{j=1}^d Q(v_j, p_j)$, we have the vector form of (2.7),

$$\phi_v(v) = \min_p Q_v(v, p) + \sum_{j=1}^d \varphi(p_j). \tag{2.8}$$

By substituting (2.8) into (2.6), we obtain that

$$\min_v \{\phi_v(v) + J(v)\} = \min_{v,p} \{Q_v(v, p) + \sum_{j=1}^d \varphi(p_j) + J(v)\}, \tag{2.9}$$

where p_j is determined by a minimization function $\delta(.)$ that is only related to $\phi(.)$ (See Table 2.2 for specific forms). In HQ optimization, $\delta(.)$ is derived from conjugate function and satisfies that $\{Q(v_j, \delta(v_j)) + \varphi(\delta(v_j))\} \leq \{Q(v_j, p_j) + \varphi(p_j)\}$. Let $\delta_v(v) \doteq [\delta(v_1), \dots, \delta(v_d)]$, and then one can alternately minimize (2.9) as follows,

$$p^{t+1} = \delta_v(v), \tag{2.10}$$

$$v^{t+1} = \arg\min_v Q_v(v, p^{t+1}) + J(v), \tag{2.11}$$

where t indicates the tth iteration. Algorithm 1 summarizes the optimization procedure. At each step, the objective function in (2.9) is employed with respect to a single parameter variable alternatively until it converges.

2.2.2 The Additive and Multiplicative Forms

In HQ minimization, the half-quadratic reformulation $Q(v_j, p_j)$ of an original cost-function has two forms [54,55]: the additive form denoted by $Q_A(v_j, p_j)$ and the multiplicative form denoted by $Q_M(v_j, p_j)$. Specifically, $Q_A(v_j, p_j)$ is formulated as [55],

---

Algorithm 1 Half-Quadratic Based Algorithms

1: **Input:**data matrix X, test sample y, and $v = 0$.
2: **Output:**v
3: **while** "not converged" **do**
4:    $p^{t+1} = \delta_v(v)$
5:    $v^{t+1} = \arg\min\limits_{v} Q_v(v, p^{t+1}) + J(v)$
6:    $t = t + 1$
7: **end while**

$$Q_A(v_j, p_j) = (v_j\sqrt{c} - p_j/\sqrt{c})^2, \tag{2.12}$$

where c is a constant and $c > 0$. The additive form indicates that we can expand a function $\phi(.)$ to a combination of quadratic terms and the auxiliary variable p_j is related to v_j. During iterative minimization, the value of v_j is updated and refined by p_j. If a potential function $\phi(.)$ satisfies,

(a) $t \to \phi(t)$ is convex;
(b) $c > 0$ is such that $t \to \{ct^2/2 - \phi(t)\}$ is convex;
(c) $\phi(t) = \phi(-t), \forall v \in r$;
(d) ϕ is continuous on R;
(e) $\lim\limits_{|t| \to \infty} \phi(t)/t^2 < c/2$,

then there is a minimization function $\delta_A(t) = ct - \phi'(t)$ such that [112]

$$\delta_A(t) = \arg\min\limits_{w}(t\sqrt{c} - w/\sqrt{c})^2 + \varphi(w). \tag{2.13}$$

Let $c = 1$, (2.13) takes the form,

$$\delta_A(t) = \arg\min\limits_{w}(t - w)^2 + \varphi(w). \tag{2.14}$$

In the two-step iterative shrinkage/thresholding algorithms [161], the minimization function of (2.13) is also known as proximal mapping [9, 30]. And when $\phi(.)$ is Huber M-estimator, the following additive form holds:

$$\phi_H^\lambda(t) = \min\limits_{w}\{(t - w)^2 + \lambda|w|\}, \tag{2.15}$$

where absolute function $\lambda|w|$ is the dual potential function of Huber M-estimator $\phi_H^\lambda(.)$.
The multiplicative form $Q_M(v_j, p_j)$ is formulated in the form [54]

$$Q_M(v_j, p_j) = \frac{1}{2}p_j v_j^2. \tag{2.16}$$

It indicates that we can expand a non-convex (or convex) function $\phi(.)$ to the quadratic term of the multiplicative form. The auxiliary variable p_j is introduced as a data-fidelity term. For v_j, p_j indicates the contribution of v_j to the whole data v. In addition, if a potential function $\phi(.)$ satisfies the following conditions ($t = v_j$ and $w = p_j$),

(a) $\forall t, \phi(t) \geq 0, \phi(0) = 0$;
(b) $\phi(t) = \phi(-t)$;
(c) $\phi(.)$ continuously differentiable;
(d) $\forall t, \phi'(t) \geq 0$;
(e) $\phi'(t)/2t$ continuous and strictly decreasing on $[0, +\infty]$;
(f) $\lim\limits_{t \to +\infty} \{\phi'(t)/2t\} = 0$;
(g) $\lim\limits_{t \to 0^+} \{\phi'(t)/2t\} = M, 0 < M < +\infty$,

then Theorem 2.1 holds.

Theorem 2.1 ([22]). *Let $\phi(.)$ be a potential function that satisfies the above seven conditions, then*

(a) there exists a strictly convex and decreasing dual function $\varphi : (0, M] \to [0, \beta)$, where

$$\beta = \lim\limits_{t \to +\infty} \left(\phi(t) - t^2(\phi'(t)/2t)\right),$$

such that

$$\phi(t) = \inf\limits_{0 < w \leq M} (wt^2 + \varphi(w)),$$

(b) for every fixed $t \geq 0$, the value $\hat{w}$ for which the minimum is reached, i.e., such that

$$\inf\limits_{0 < w \leq M} (wt^2 + \varphi(w)) = (\hat{w}t^2 + \varphi(\hat{w})),$$

is unique and given by the following minimization function

$$\hat{w} = \delta_M(t) = \phi'(t)/2t.$$

Table 2.2 tabulates five commonly used half-quadratic functions and their corresponding minimization functions. We observe that these functions have similar properties and achieve the minima (zero) at origin. They all belong to M-estimator in Sect. 2.1 and naturally robust to outliers. ℓ_1-ℓ_2 potential function takes both the advantage of absolute function ($|.|$) to reduce the influence of large errors and that of ℓ estimator (t^2) to be continuous. "Fair" potential function defines continuous derivatives of the first three orders and yields a unique solution. "Log-cosh" potential function is a strictly convex function and is an approximation of Huber

Table 2.2 Minimization functions δ relevant to the multiplicative and the additive form of HQ for different potential functions ϕ. α in M-estimator is a constant

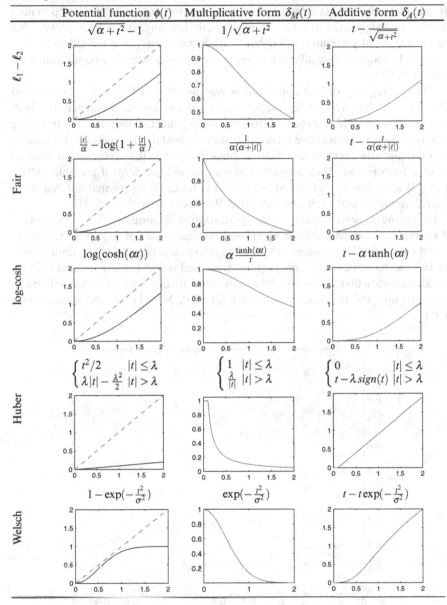

	Potential function $\phi(t)$	Multiplicative form $\delta_M(t)$	Additive form $\delta_A(t)$
$\ell_1 - \ell_2$	$\sqrt{\alpha + t^2} - 1$	$1/\sqrt{\alpha + t^2}$	$t - \dfrac{t}{\sqrt{\alpha + t^2}}$
Fair	$\dfrac{|t|}{\alpha} - \log\left(1 + \dfrac{|t|}{\alpha}\right)$	$\dfrac{1}{\alpha(\alpha + |t|)}$	$t - \dfrac{t}{\alpha(\alpha + |t|)}$
log-cosh	$\log(\cosh(\alpha t))$	$\alpha\dfrac{\tanh(\alpha t)}{t}$	$t - \alpha\tanh(\alpha t)$
Huber	$\begin{cases} t^2/2 & |t| \leq \lambda \\ \lambda|t| - \dfrac{\lambda^2}{2} & |t| > \lambda \end{cases}$	$\begin{cases} 1 & |t| \leq \lambda \\ \dfrac{\lambda}{|t|} & |t| > \lambda \end{cases}$	$\begin{cases} 0 & |t| \leq \lambda \\ t - \lambda\,\mathrm{sign}(t) & |t| > \lambda \end{cases}$
Welsch	$1 - \exp(-\dfrac{t^2}{\sigma^2})$	$\exp(-\dfrac{t^2}{\sigma^2})$	$t - t\exp(-\dfrac{t^2}{\sigma^2})$

potential function [77], which is a parabola in the vicinity of zero and increases linearly at a given level $|t| > \lambda$. Angst et al. [4] show that Huber function can efficiently handle outliers than ℓ_1 estimator for motion problems. "Welsch" potential function is widely used in information theoretic learning. It has been proved that the robustness of correntropy [99] based algorithms is actually related to Welsch function. In addition, they all can be used as an approximator of ℓ_0-norm to enhance sparsity [69].

The convergency of HQ optimization was justified in [3, 112]. Nikolova and NG [112] further derived the upper bound of the root-convergence for both multiplicative and additive reformulations, showing that the bound of multiplicative form is lower than the additive form. Also, they showed that the number of iterations for multiplicative form is less than additive form, but the computation time of additive form is less. They suggested to use the additive form if possible. Allain et al. [3] also showed that the additive form is faster. They pointed out that these algorithms are special cases of generalized Weiszfeld algorithms [152].

Interestingly, some widely used optimization algorithms, e.g., the robust M-estimator and mean-shift, can be viewed as special cases of HQ optimization. As is well known that HQ remains a local minimization algorithm. Global minimization via HQ can be achieved by applying the graduated non-convexity method [12] for visual reconstruction. Now HQ is widely used in the field of penalized image reconstruction and restoration, such as SAR [20], MRI [132], and spectrometry [105].

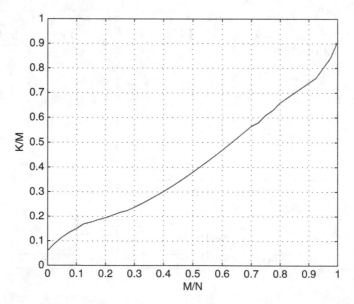

Fig. 2.2 Phase transition diagram corresponding to a compressed sensing or robust system where A is the random Gaussian matrix. The boundary separates regions in the problem space. Below the boundary, signal is well reconstructed; and above the boundary, the system lacks sparsity or robustness, and/or too few measurements are obtained to solve the reconstruction problem correctly [42, 44, 118]

2.3   Phase Transition Diagrams

Phase transition diagrams are often used to evaluate a robust or compressed sensing system [42, 44]. Given a particular system, governed by a sensing matrix A, let $\delta = M/N$ be a normalized measure of under-sampling factor and $\rho = K/M$ be a normalized measure of sparsity or robustness. M, N, and K indicate the number of features, the number of samples, and the number of nonzero entries (or the number of corrupted entries), respectively. A plot of the pairing of the variables δ and ρ describes a 2D phase space $(\delta, \rho) \in [0, 1]$. It has been shown that for many practical sensing matrices, there are sharp boundaries in this phase space. These boundaries clearly divide the solvable problems from unsolvable one in noiseless case. That is, a phase transition diagram provides a way of checking sparsity or robustness, indicating how sparsity and robustness affect the success of a system. Figure 2.2 gives an example of a phase transition diagram which is obtained when sensing matrix A is a random Gaussian matrix. Below the boundary, signal is well reconstructed; and above the boundary, the system lacks sparsity or robustness, and/or too few measurements are obtained to solve the reconstruction problem correctly [118].

2.4   Summary

In this chapter, some preliminary theory and methods related to information theoretic learning have been studied. M-estimation has a long history in robust statistics, which provides a theoretic tool to analyze robustness of information theoretic loss functions. To systematically evaluate algorithmic robustness, phase transition diagram [42, 44] has been introduced, which is a novel and important research trend in compressed sensing. One of merits of information measures is the inclusion of second and higher order information, which also makes these measures difficult to be solved. Many algorithms [59, 99, 107] have been proposed to simplify the optimization of these measures. Half-quadratic optimization, including the additive and multiplicative forms, has been proved to be an efficient tool to optimize information theoretic measures. One future direction of half-quadratic optimization is developing accelerated algorithms (especially for non-convex loss functions) to save computational costs. Refer to [26, 151] for recent advances of these algorithms.

Chapter 3
Information Measures

Information theoretic learning (ITL) was initiated in the late 1990s at CNEL [126]. It uses descriptors from information theory (entropy and divergences) estimated directly from the data to substitute the conventional statistical descriptors of variance and covariance. It can be used in the adaptation of linear or nonlinear filters and also in unsupervised and supervised machine learning applications. In this chapter, we introduce two commonly used differential entropies for data understanding and information theoretic measures (ITMs) for evaluations in abstaining classifications.

3.1 Shannon Entropy

Let $X = [x_1, \cdots, x_n] \in R^{d \times n}$ be a set of n data samples and $U = [u_1, \cdots, u_m] \in R^{d \times m}$ be an orthonormal projection matrix whose columns constitute the bases of an m-dimensional subspace. The Shannon entropy of a dataset X with probability density function (PDF) $f_X(x)$ is defined by

$$H(X) = -\int \log(f_X(x)) f_X(x) dx. \tag{3.1}$$

If $f_X(x)$ is a Gaussian distribution as

$$G_X(x, \mu, \Sigma) \triangleq \frac{1}{(2\pi)^{k/2} |\Sigma|^{1/2}} \exp(-\tfrac{1}{2}(x-\mu)^T \Sigma^{-1}(x-\mu)), \tag{3.2}$$

where μ is the mean and $\Sigma = E(x - \mu)^2$ is the covariance matrix of X, the estimate of entropy is obtained as [31]

$$H(X) = \log(|\Sigma|) + \frac{d}{2} \log 2\pi + \frac{d}{2}, \tag{3.3}$$

where $|.|$ is the absolute value of determinant [31, p. 254].

© The Author(s) 2014
R. He et al., *Robust Recognition via Information Theoretic Learning*,
SpringerBriefs in Computer Science, DOI 10.1007/978-3-319-07416-0_3

In most real-world applications, data are often drawn from non-Gaussian distribution. It is necessary to consider the entropy under non-Gaussian distribution. Here we use Gaussian mixture model (GMM) to approximate the data's distribution. In statistics, GMM is a probability distribution that is a convex combination of single-Gaussian probability distribution [23]:

$$f_X(x) \triangleq \sum_{k=1}^{K} a_k G_X(x, \mu_k, \Sigma_k), \tag{3.4}$$

where $0 \le a_k \le 1$, $a_1 + \ldots + a_K = 1$ and K is the number of Gaussian components. Each Σ_k can be approximately estimated by the part of data X, i.e.,

$$\Sigma_k \approx X_k(I - \tfrac{ee^T}{e^T e})(I - \tfrac{ee^T}{e^T e})^T X_k^T = X_k(I - \tfrac{ee^T}{e^T e})X_k^T, \tag{3.5}$$

where e is all-one column vector, $X_k = XS_k$, and S_k is a selection matrix to select part of X (i.e., $XS_k = \{x_{k1}, x_{k2}, \ldots, x_{kl}\}$ are always selected from $X = \{x_1, \ldots, x_n\}$). We introduce a new notation L_k as:

$$L_k = S_k(I - \tfrac{ee^T}{e^T e})S_k^T. \tag{3.6}$$

Then Σ_k has the following formulation:

$$\Sigma_k \approx XL_kX^T. \tag{3.7}$$

Considering the entropy based on GMM, we have following theorems.

Theorem 3.1 ([74]). *The Shannon entropy is invariant under orthonormal linear transformations, i.e.,*

$$H(U^T X) = H(X), \tag{3.8}$$

where $U \in R^{d \times d}$ and $U^T U = I$.

Proof. According to properties of differential entropy [31], we have

$$H(U^T X) = H(X) + \log(|U^T|). \tag{3.9}$$

Because U is an orthonormal matrix, we can obtain $\log(|U^T|) = 0$; hence,

$$H(U^T X) = H(X) + \log(|U^T|) = H(X). \tag{3.10}$$

$\square$

Rotational invariance is a fundamental property of Euclidean space with ℓ_2-norm. It has been emphasized in the context of learning algorithms [29]. For any orthonormal coordinate rotation, data transformation U is invariant on ℓ_2-norm, i.e., $||U^T x||_2 = ||x||^2$. Theorem 3.1 illustrates that the entropy is also invariant to rotation. It is independent of the selection of a coordinate system for dimensionality reduction.

Theorem 3.2 ([74]). *The Shannon entropy is bounded under orthonormal linear transformations, i.e.,*

$$0 \leq H(U_F^T X) \leq H(X), \tag{3.11}$$

where $U_F^T : R^d \to R^m$, $m < d$ and $U_F^T U_F = I$.

Proof. Let $U_B \in R^{d \times (d-m)}$ be a matrix whose columns constitute the complement subspace of U_F, and define a matrix U as

$$U = [U_F \quad U_B] \quad , U^T X = [U_F^T X \quad U_B^T X]. \tag{3.12}$$

Since U is a $d \times d$ orthonormal matrix, it follows from Theorem 3.1 that $H(X) = H(U^T X)$. Considering that $H(X) \geq 0$ and the chain rule for entropies [31, p. 22], we have

$$H(X) = H(U_F^T X U_B^T X) = H(U_F^T X) + H(U_B^T X | U_F^T X) \geq H(U_F^T X). \tag{3.13}$$

Hence

$$0 \leq H(U_F^T X) \leq H(X).$$

$\square$

Theorem 3.2 states that the entropy of orthonormal subspace of the original feature space is bounded. The information uncertainty reduces after dimensionality reduction. The minimum entropy (entropy is zero) is achieved when all data collapse into a single point and then there is no uncertainty.

Theorem 3.3 ([74] Bound of Shannon entropy based on GMM). *If data is drawn from GMM, an upper bound of Shannon entropy is*

$$H(f_X(x)) \leq \frac{1}{2} \log((2\pi)^n \sum_{k=1}^{K} a_k |\Sigma_k|) + H_G, \tag{3.14}$$

where

$$H_G = \frac{1}{2} \sum_{k=1}^{K} a_k \int f_X(x)(x - \mu_k)^T \Sigma_k^{-1}(x - \mu_k) dx. \tag{3.15}$$

Proof. Since $\log(x)$ is a strictly concave function of x and $a_1 + \ldots + a_K = 1$, we obtain

$$H(f_X(x)) = -\int f_X(x)\log f_X(x)dx$$

$$\leq -\int f_X(x)\sum_{k=1}^{K}a_k\log(G(x,\mu_k,\Sigma_k))dx$$

$$= -\sum_{k=1}^{K}a_k\int f_X(x)\log(G(x,\mu_k,\Sigma_k))dx$$

$$= -\sum_{k=1}^{K}a_k\int f_X(x)[-\frac{1}{2}(x-\mu_k)^T\Sigma_k^{-1}(x-\mu_k)-\log((\sqrt{2\pi})^n|\Sigma_k|^{\frac{1}{2}})]dx$$

$$= \frac{1}{2}\sum_{k=1}^{K}a_k\int f_X(x)(x-\mu_k)^T\Sigma_k^{-1}(x-\mu_k)dx+\frac{1}{2}\sum_{k=1}^{K}a_k\log((2\pi)^n|\Sigma_k|)$$

$$= H_G+\frac{1}{2}\sum_{k=1}^{K}a_k\log((2\pi)^n|\Sigma_k|)\leq\frac{1}{2}\log((2\pi)^n\sum_{k=1}^{K}a_k|\Sigma_k|)+H_G$$

$$\square$$

Theorem 3.3 gives an upper bound of entropy based on GMM. Then the entropy can be minimized via this upper bound. Based on Theorem 3.3, a minimum entropy linear embedding (mELE) method is developed for data understanding [74]. Hou and He [74] give a 3D synthetic data to demonstrate mELE and other three linear embedding methods, including principal component analysis (PCA) [119], independent component analysis (ICA) [79], and locality preserving projections (LPP) [70]. The synthetic data is generated by

$$\begin{cases} x=t \\ y=\sin(4t) \\ z=x^2+y^2 \end{cases} \tag{3.16}$$

where

$$t\sim N(0,1) \quad \text{is a Gaussian distribution.} \tag{3.17}$$

Figure 3.1 shows the synthetic data under different Gaussian assumptions in 3D. And Fig. 3.2 shows the optimal 2D subspaces of four linear embedding methods on Gaussian distribution sampling. Since the data points in original space are dense close to the center and sparse close to the boundary, the dimensional reduction results of PCA and ICA are significantly different from those of LPP and mELE. And the results of LPP and mELE are similar to the curve of sin function in (3.16), which indicates that both of them give a better understanding of the original 3D data.

Fig. 3.1 Synthetic data under
Gaussian distribution in 3D
[74]

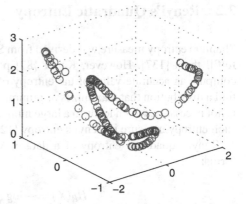

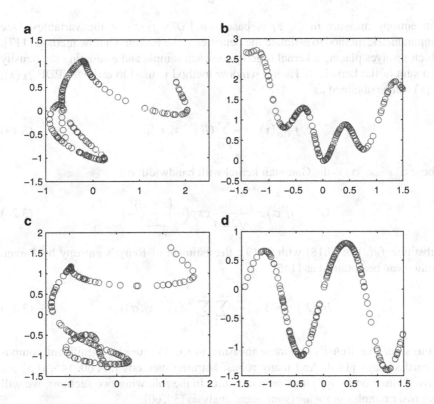

Fig. 3.2 Optimal 2D subspaces of different algorithms on Gaussian distribution assumption
(**a**) PCA, (**b**) LPP, (**c**) ICA, and (**d**) mELE

3.2   Renyi's Quadratic Entropy

Shannon entropy measure was derived from Shannon's three axioms so that it should fulfill them [137]. However, Kapur [87] pointed out that whenthe aim is not to compute an accurate value of the entropy of a particular distribution, but rather to find a distribution that maximizes or minimizes entropy, then Shannon's third axiom is not necessary, which leads to a large number of alternative entropy measures. One such entropy measure is Renyi's entropy [129].

Renyi's quadratic entropy of a dataset X with PDF $f_X(x)$ takes the following forms:

$$H_R(X) = -\log \int f_X^2(x)dx. \tag{3.18}$$

The entropy measure in (3.18) is based on PDFs $f_X(x)$ of the variables. One nonparametric method to estimate the densities is the Parzen window method [117], which involves placing a kernel function on each sample and evaluating the density as a sum of the kernels. If Parzen window method is used to estimate PDF $f_X(x)$, $f_X(x)$ can be obtained as

$$\widehat{f}_{X;\sigma}(x) = \frac{1}{n} \sum_{i=1}^{n} G(x - x_i, \sigma), \tag{3.19}$$

where $G(x - x_i, \sigma)$ is the Gaussian kernel with bandwidth σ

$$G(x - x_i, \sigma) = \frac{1}{\sqrt{2\pi}\sigma} \exp(-\frac{(x - x_i)^2}{2\sigma^2}). \tag{3.20}$$

Substitute $f_X(x)$ in (3.18) with (3.19); the estimate of Renyi's entropy by Parzen method can be obtained as [145]

$$H_R(X) = -\log(\frac{1}{n^2} \sum_{i=1}^{n} \sum_{j=1}^{n} G(x_j - x_i, \sigma)). \tag{3.21}$$

It turns out that Renyi's quadratic measure in (3.21) provides significant computational savings [145]. And many robust learning methods [59, 60, 145, 165] are derived based on Renyi's quadratic measure. In the following two sections, we will give two examples in robust component analysis [59, 60].

3.2.1   Robust PCA

Subspace learning has been a fundamental problem in the studies of machine learning and computer vision. It is a common preprocessing step to learn a low-dimensional data representation from the raw input variables which might be strongly relevant and redundant [57]. It plays an important role in many learning tasks where high dimensionality is a big challenge [47].

From different standpoints, there are two major categories of subspace learning: unsupervised and supervised. In unsupervised subspace learning, the data class labels are unknown. The best-known representative of unsupervised methods is PCA [73]. In supervised subspace learning, the information of class labels is incorporated to learn a low-dimensional representation where the class differences are maximized, so that a discriminator can be learned in the subspace [144]. The linear discriminant analysis (LDA) [7] is the most representative one among these discriminators. Since PCA and LDA are based on mean square errors, they are all sensitive to outliers [59, 60]. In addition, both PCA and LDA assume that data are drawn from Gaussian distribution.

3.2.1.1 Principal Component Analysis

Consider a dataset of samples $X = [x_1, \cdots, x_n]$ where x_i is a variable with dimensionality d, $U = [u_1, \cdots, u_m] \in R^{d \times m}$ is a projection matrix whose columns constitute the bases of an m-dimensional subspace, and $V = [v_1, \cdots, v_n] \in R^{m \times n}$ is the projection coordinates under the projection matrix U.

PCA can be defined as an orthogonal projection of the samples onto a lower dimensional subspace such that the variance of the projected data is maximized [73]. Equivalently, it can also be defined as an orthogonal projection that minimizes the average reconstruction error, which is the mean-squared distance between the samples and their projections [119].

From reconstruction error point of view, PCA can be formulated as the following optimization problem:

$$\min_{U,V} \sum_{i=1}^{n} ||x_i - (\mu + Uv_i)||^2, \tag{3.22}$$

where μ is the center of X. The optimization problem in (3.22) can also be written below:

$$\min_{U,V} \sum_{i=1}^{n} \sum_{j=1}^{d} (x_{ij} - (\mu_{ij} + \sum_{p=1}^{m} v_{ip} u_{pj}))^2. \tag{3.23}$$

By projection theorem [100], for a fixed U, V that minimizes (3.22) is uniquely determined by $V = U^T X$ and superscript T denotes matrix transposition. Because (3.22.) is based on ℓ_2-norm (Euclidean distance), the PCA is often denoted as ℓ_2-PCA. In order to develop a fast and robust subspace algorithm, the expectation maximization (EM) algorithm [2, 134] and fixed-point algorithm are developed to solve (3.23).

The global minimum of (3.22) is provided by singular value decomposition (SVD) [56], whose optimal solution is also the solution of the following alternative formulation of PCA:

$$\max_{U^T U = I} Tr(U^T \Sigma U), \qquad (3.24)$$

where $\Sigma = \sum_{i=1}^{n} (x_i - \mu)(x_i - \mu)^T$ is the covariance matrix , $Tr(.)$ is the matrix trace operation, and T denotes the transpose. Equation (3.24) searches for a projection matrix where the variances of $U^T X$ are maximized. Based on (3.24), PCA can also be further unified in the patch alignment framework [169].

In graph embedding (GE) framework [160], PCA can also be formulated as the following optimization problem:

$$\max_{U^T U = I} Tr(U^T X (I - W) X^T U), \qquad (3.25)$$

where I is the identity matrix and W is a $n \times n$ matrix whose elements are all equal to $1/n$. The solutions of PCA can be obtained by solving the following eigenvalue decomposition problem:

$$X(I - W)X^T u = \lambda u. \qquad (3.26)$$

In graph embedding, the matrix $L = I - W$ is often denoted as Laplacian matrix.

3.2.1.2 MaxEnt-PCA

The aim of MaxEnt-PCA is to learn a new data distribution in a subspace such that entropy is maximized. Here we consider the Renyi's quadratic entropy in (3.21) to develop a robust and high-order PCA.

In unsupervised subspace learning, one considers the following constraint MaxEnt problem:

$$\max_{U} H_R(U^T X) \quad s.t. \quad U^T U = I. \qquad (3.27)$$

Note that the orthonormal constraint is necessary and important for extracting non-redundant features. When the formula of $f_X(x)$ is given, the MaxEnt distribution about $f_{U^T X}(x)$ in (3.27) is only relative to the subspace U. When Parzen window density estimation of entropy in (3.21) is adopted, the optimization problem in (3.27) takes the form

$$\max_{U} \left(-\log\left(\frac{1}{n^2} \sum_{i=1}^{n} \sum_{j=1}^{n} G(U^T x_j - U^T x_i, \sigma^2)\right)\right) \qquad (3.28)$$

$$s.t. \quad U^T U = I$$

We denote the above method as MaxEnt-PCA. From the entropy point of view, MaxEnt-PCA is a natural extension of PCA from Gaussian distribution assumption to Parzen window density estimation. Obviously the superiority of MaxEnt-PCA lies in the nonparametric density estimation from training dataset, which can be more flexible and robust.

Furthermore, it is obvious that (3.28) can be viewed as a robust *M-estimator* [77] formulation of scatter matrix in (3.25) with robust Welsch M-estimator $r(x) = 1 - exp(-x^2)$ [77]. Therefore MaxEnt-PCA can be viewed as a robust extension of the classical PCA.

3.2.1.3 Algorithm of MaxEnt-PCA

Proposition 3.1. *The optimal solution of MaxEnt-PCA in (3.28) is given by the eigenvectors of the following generalized eigen-decomposition problem:*

$$XL(U)X^T U = 2U\Lambda, \tag{3.29}$$

where

$$L(U) = D(U) - W(U) \tag{3.30}$$

$$W_{ij}(U) = \frac{G(U^T x_i - U^T x_j, \sigma^2)}{\sigma^2 \sum_{i=1}^{n} \sum_{j=1}^{n} G(U^T x_i - U^T x_j, \sigma^2)} \tag{3.31}$$

$$D_{ii}(U) = \sum_{j=1}^{n} W_{ij}(U). \tag{3.32}$$

This can be figured out by applying the Lagrangian factor on (3.28), where entries of Λ are the Lagrangian coefficients associated to the orthonormal constraint on U as follows:

$$J_H \overset{\Delta}{=} -\log \frac{1}{n^2} \sum_{i=1}^{n} \sum_{j=1}^{n} G(U^T x_i - U^T x_j, \sigma^2) - Tr(\Lambda(U^T U - I))$$

where $Tr(.)$ is the matrix trace operation. The KKT condition for optimal solution specifies that the derivative of J_H with respect to U must be zero:

$$\frac{\partial J_H}{\partial U} = \sum_{i=1}^{n} \sum_{j=1}^{n} W_{ij}(U)(x_i - x_j)(x_i^T - x_j^T)U - 2U\Lambda = 0$$

Then we have

$$XL(U)X^T U = 2U\Lambda. \tag{3.33}$$

Intuitively, an optimal U is the eigenvector of the symmetric matrix $XL(U)X^T$ and the Lagrangian multiplier Λ then becomes a diagonal matrix: $\Lambda = diag(\lambda_1, \ldots, \lambda_m)$.

In Proposition 3.1, $W_{ij}(U)$ is an approximation of probability distribution on x_i under the jth Parzen estimate, and the $D_{ii}(U)$ is an approximation of probability value on x_i under the ith Parzen estimate. We follow the notation of graph embedding and denote $W(U)$ and $L(U)$ as Parzen probability matrix and Laplacian probability matrix, respectively. Compared to (3.26), MaxEnt-PCA is actually a special weighted PCA. However, PCA is based on Gaussian assumption, while MaxEnt-PCA is derived from Parzen estimation.

Since $L(U)$ in (3.29) is also a function of U, the eigenvalue decomposition problem in (3.29) has no closed-form solution. Fortunately, we can solve this MaxEnt problem by gradient-based fixed-point algorithm [38, 78, 138] which is often used in subspace learning. As a result, we use the following steps to update the projection matrix U:

$$U = (I + \beta XL(U)X^T)U \tag{3.34}$$

$$U = svd(U) \tag{3.35}$$

where β is a step length to ensure an increment of the objective function and $svd(U)$ returns an orthonormal base by the SVD on matrix U. In (3.34), the U is updated by the gradient direction. In (3.35), an orthonormal solution of U is obtained. The convergence of the fixed-point algorithm is actually guaranteed by [38, 56].

The fixed-point algorithm of MaxEnt-PCA is outlined in Algorithm 2.[1] The step length β can be decided by the line search method [13]. Note that the estimate of $f_X(x)$ is performed on the reduced dimension instead of original input feature space. The bandwidth σ is an important parameter in MaxEnt-PCA, which is used in Parzen estimate of $f_X(x)$. Considering the theoretical analysis of nonparametric entropy estimators [82, 127], we present a tunable way to set the bandwidth as a factor of average distance between projected samples:

$$\sigma^2 = \frac{1}{sn^2} \sum_{i=1}^{n} \sum_{j=1}^{n} ||U^T x_i - U^T x_j||^2, \tag{3.36}$$

where s is a scale factor. The bandwidth σ is also a function of subspace U. In each update, the bandwidth σ is also updated on the projection dataset $U^T X$.

---

[1]Code: http://www.openpr.org.cn/index.php/Download/.

Algorithm 2 MaxEnt-PCA

 1: **Input:** data matrix X, random orthonormal matrix U and a small positive value ε
 2: **Output:** orthonormal matrix U
 3: **repeat**
 4:    Initialize converged = FALSE.
 5:    Calculate σ according to (3.36), and $L(U)$ according to (3.30)
 6:    Select a suitable β , and update U according to (3.34) and (3.35)
 7:    **if** the entropy delta is smaller than ε **then**
 8:       converged = TRUE
 9:    **end if**
10: **until** converged==TRUE

During each update in MaxEnt-PCA, the probability distribution is estimated by the Parzen method. Since an outlier is far away from the data cluster, its contribution to estimation of the PDF will be smaller so that it always receives a low value in the Parzen probability matrix W. Therefore, outliers will have weaker influence on the estimation of the MaxEnt probability distribution as entropy increases. Hence, MaxEnt-PCA is robust against outliers.

3.2.1.4 Numerical Results on UCI Balance Scale Dataset

In this subsection, UCI balance scale dataset was selected to demonstrate the iterative procedure of MaxEnt-PCA as well as to discuss the relationships and differences between PCA.

The balance scale dataset [111] is a benchmark data set and is frequently used to verify the effectiveness of subspace learning algorithms. It consists of 625 examples in three categories. The numbers of instances in all three categories are 288, 288, and 49, respectively. Each instance has four raw attributes, i.e., left-weight, left-distance, right-weight, and right-distance. Each dimension of raw data is normalized (with zero mean and standard variance). The data were projected into a two-dimensional subspace for visualization.

Figure 3.3a plots the scatter of data with the first three dimensions. We see that the data were arranged in 25 clusters. And Fig. 3.3b shows the 2D scatterplots of PCA. Obviously, it is difficult to directly predict the high-dimensional structure of the balance scale dataset. Figure 3.3c, d further depicts the visualization results of MaxEnt-PCA after the 10th and 30th iterations, respectively. After 10 iterations, the data distribution becomes similar to the real data distribution. After 30 iterations, the data clusters in 25 groups and the margins between different groups were maximized. From Fig. 3.3, we can learn that Renyi's quadratic entropy is helpful for discovering the intrinsic structure of high-dimensional data.

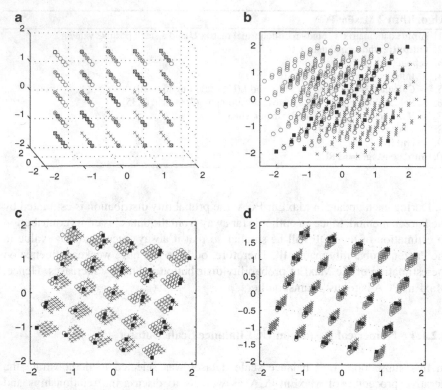

Fig. 3.3 Visualization results of PCA and MaxEnt-PCA on the balance scale dataset. (**a**) Scatterplot of the Balance dataset, (**b**) scatterplot of PCA, (**c**) after the tenth iteration of MaxEnt-PCA, and (**d**) after the 30th iteration of MaxEnt-PCA

3.2.2 Robust Discriminant Analysis

In this section, we investigate robust discriminative analysis problem based on Renyi's quadratic entropy. The training sample set is assumed to be represented as a matrix $X = [x_1, \ldots, x_n] \in \mathbb{R}^{m \times n}$, where n is the sample number and m is the original feature dimension. The class label indicator information of the training data is denoted by the matrix $C = [c_1, \ldots, c_n] \in \mathbb{R}^{n_c \times n}$, where n_c is the number of classes and the elements of the indicator vector c_i are set to be 1 or 0, according to whether x_i is drawn from the jth class. In practice, the feature dimension m is usually very high and thus it is necessary and beneficial to transform the data from the original high-dimensional space to a low-dimensional one for alleviating the curse of dimensionality. The purpose of linear discriminative analysis is to search for a projection matrix $W \in \mathbb{R}^{m' \times m}$ that transforms $x_i \in \mathbb{R}^m$ into a desired low-dimensional representation $y_i \in \mathbb{R}^{m'}$, where $m' \ll m$ and $y_i = W x_i$.

According to Renyi's quadratic entropy $H_R(X)$ in (3.21), we arrive at the following formulation:

$$\hat{H}_R(X) = -\log \hat{V}(X) + \text{const.}$$

$$\hat{V}(X) = \sum_{i=1}^{n} \sum_{j=1}^{n} g(x_i - x_j, \sqrt{2}\sigma).$$

where $g(x - x', \sigma) = \exp(-\|x - x'\|^2/\sigma^2)$. $\hat{V}(X)$ is known as the *information potential* (IP) of the set X which is an analogy borrowed from physics for potential of group of interacting particles [124]. Intuitively, the more regular set X is, the higher $\hat{V}(X)$ will be.

Following similar arguments, one can derive the equations for Renyi's *cross-entropy* between two sets X and X' as follows:

$$\hat{H}_R(X; X') = -\log \hat{V}(X; X') + \text{const.}$$

$$\hat{V}(X; X') = \sum_{i=1}^{n} \sum_{j=1}^{n} g(x_i - x'_j, \sqrt{2}\sigma).$$

Intuitively, the cross IP $\hat{V}(X; X')$ reflects the extent of correlation between set X and X'.

Next, based on the above two IPs $\hat{V}(X)$ and $\hat{V}(X; X')$, we build a framework of robust linear discriminative analysis.

3.2.2.1 Problem Formulation

We consider the projection matrix $W \in \mathbb{R}^{n_c \times m}$ that maps X into an $n_c \times n$ matrix $Y = WX$. The following criterion is used to encode the IP of feature Y and the cross IP between Y and the class label C:

$$E(W) = (1 - \lambda)\hat{V}(WX) + \lambda \hat{V}(WX; C) \tag{3.37}$$

where λ is a tunable trade-off parameter. The parameter W that maximizes $E(W)$ is desirable in the sense of minimizing the entropy of training set (reflected by the first unsupervised term), while separating training samples with different labels (reflected by the second supervised term). For a better statistical interpretation (see Sect. 3.2.2.2) of (3.37), we ignore the between class feature-label intersections contained in the term $\hat{V}(WX; C)$; thus the problem is finally formulated as

$$W^* = \arg\max_{W} \hat{E}(W)$$

$$= \underset{W}{\arg\max} \ (1 - \lambda) \sum_{i=1}^{n} \sum_{j=1}^{N} g(Wx_i - Wx_j, \sqrt{2}\sigma)$$

$$+ \lambda \sum_{i=1}^{N} l_i g(Wx_i - c_i, \sqrt{2}\sigma) - \gamma \|W\|^2 \tag{3.38}$$

where l_i is the size of the class x_i belongs to and term $\gamma \|W\|^2$ is the introduced Tikhonov regularization (with Frobenius norm) to avoid the possible over-fitting to training data.

We conventionally choose class label indicator as each column of the response C in (3.38). Actually, as pointed out in [15], C can be more generally learnt via some graph embedding algorithms, e.g., LDA and LPP, with different dimensions m'. Especially, when $m' = n_c$, the learnt spectral response C by LDA is equivalent to the one used here.

3.2.2.2 Robustness Justification

Let $\lambda = 1$ and $\gamma = 0$ in (3.38); we get

$$W^* = \underset{W}{\arg\max} \sum_{i=1}^{n} l_i g(Wx_i - c_i, \sqrt{2}\sigma)$$

$$= \underset{W}{\arg\min} \sum_{i=1}^{n} l_i \rho \left(\frac{Wx_i - c_i}{\sqrt{2}\sigma} \right) \tag{3.39}$$

where $\rho(u) = -\exp(-u^2)$. It is obvious that (3.39) is a robust *M-estimator* [77] formulation of the recently developed spectral regression discriminant analysis (SRDA) [15], with regressor X, observation C, regression parameter W, and loss function $\rho(u)$. Moreover, $\rho(u)$ satisfies $\lim_{|u|\to\infty} \rho'(u) = 0$; thus it also belongs to the so-called redescending M-estimators [77], which have in theory some special robustness properties, e.g., the highest fixed design breakdown point. Problem (3.39) is also known as a *correntropy* [99] optimization problem.

For general cases with $0 < \lambda < 1$, the second term in the objective function (3.38) remains a redescending M-estimator of SRDA. It can be seen from Sect. 3.2.2.4 that the first term in (3.38) plays a role similar to manifold regularization used in Laplacian regularized least squares (LapRLS) [8]. Therefore, the proposed linear feature extraction formulation in (3.38) reaps the advantages of both robust statistics and manifold regularization.

3.2.2.3 Optimization

Based on the *theory of convex conjugated functions* [13], we can trivially derive the following proposition that forms the base to solve problem (3.38) in an HQ way.

Proposition 3.2 ([165]). *There exists a convex function* $\varphi : \mathbb{R} \mapsto \mathbb{R}$*, such that*

$$g(x, \sigma) = \sup_{p \in \mathbb{R}^-} \left(p \frac{\|x\|^2}{\sigma^2} - \varphi(p) \right)$$

and for a fixed x, the supremum is reached at $p = -g(x, \sigma)$.

Now we introduce the following augmented objective function in an enlarged parameter space:

$$\begin{aligned}
\hat{F}(W, P, Q) \\
= (1 - \lambda) \sum_{i,j} \left(p_{ij} \frac{\|Wx_i - Wx_j\|^2}{2\sigma^2} - \varphi(p_{ij}) \right) \\
+ \lambda \sum_i l_i \left(q_i \frac{\|Wx_i - c_i\|^2}{2\sigma^2} - \varphi(q_i) \right) \\
- \gamma \|W\|^2
\end{aligned}$$

where the $n \times n$ matrix $P = [p_{ij}]$ and Q is diagonal with entity $Q(i,i) = q_i$ storing the auxiliary variables introduced in HQ analysis. According to Proposition 3.1, we get immediately that for a fixed W, the following equation holds:

$$\hat{E}(W) = \sup_{P,Q} \hat{F}(W, P, Q).$$

It follows that

$$\max_W \hat{E}(W) = \max_{W,P,Q} \hat{F}(W, P, Q), \tag{3.40}$$

from which we can conclude that maximizing $\hat{E}(W)$ is equivalent to maximizing the augmented function $\hat{F}(W, P, Q)$ on the enlarged domain. Obviously, a local maximizer (W, P, Q) of $\hat{F}$ can be calculated in the following alternate maximization way:

$$p_{ij}^t = -g(W^{t-1}x_i - W^{t-1}x_j, \sqrt{2}\sigma), \tag{3.41}$$

$$q_i^t = -g(W^{t-1}x_i - c_i, \sqrt{2}\sigma), \tag{3.42}$$

$$W^t = \arg\max_W \text{Tr}[WX(2(1-\lambda)L_p^t + \lambda LQ^t)X^T W^T$$

$$- 2\lambda WXLQ^t C^T - \gamma WW^T], \tag{3.43}$$

where t is time stamp, matrix L is diagonal with entity $L(i,i) = l_i$, Laplacian matrix $L_p^t = D_p^t - P^t$ where D_p^t is a diagonal weight matrix whose entries are row sums of P^t, and $\mathrm{Tr}(\cdot)$ represents the matrix trace operation. We call this above three-step algorithm as *Renyi's entropy discriminant analysis* (REDA) hereafter. And the following proposition demonstrates that the alternate maximization way will converge.

Proposition 3.3. *Denote* $\hat{F}^t = \hat{F}(W^t, P^t, Q^t)$, *then the sequence* $\{\hat{F}^t\}_{t=1,2,...}$ *generated by REDA algorithm converges.*

Proof. We calculate

$$\hat{F}^t - \hat{F}^{t-1} = \left[\hat{F}(W^t, P^t, Q^t) - \hat{F}(W^{t-1}, P^t, Q^t)\right]$$
$$+ \left[\hat{F}(W^{t-1}, P^t, Q^t) - \hat{F}(W^{t-1}, P^{t-1}, Q^{t-1})\right].$$

According to (3.43) and Proposition 3.1, both terms at the right side of above equal sign are nonnegative. Therefore, the sequence $\{\hat{F}^t\}_{t=1,2,...}$ is nondecreasing. It is easy to verify that both terms in $\hat{E}(W)$ are bounded above, and thus by (3.40) we get that $\hat{F}^t$ is also bounded. Consequently we can conclude that $\{\hat{F}^t\}_{t=1,2,...}$ converges.

$\square$

3.2.2.4 Special Cases of REDA

We show that different settings of trade-off parameter λ will lead to special versions of REDA algorithm, which are highly related to the popular manifold learning algorithms LPP, SRDA, and LapRLS.

Let $\lambda = 0$ and $\gamma = 0$; the calculation of (3.43) in REDA algorithm can be equivalently rewritten as

$$W^t = \underset{WX(-D_p^1)X^TW^T=I}{\arg\min} \mathrm{Tr}[WX(-L_p^t)X^TW^T]. \tag{3.44}$$

In this formulation, we introduce an extra constraint that $WX(-D_p^1)X^TW^T = I$, where I is an identity matrix, to remove arbitrary scaling and triviality of solution, without breaking the convergence of algorithm. By initializing P^1 using the graph Laplacian [70], the calculation of W^1 is a standard LPP. When $t > 1$, (3.44) is a linear graph embedding problem with heat kernel similarity matrix $-P^t$ and constraint matrix $-D_p^1$, which can be efficiently solved via generalized eigenvalue decomposition method. We call this special version of our algorithm as REDA-LPP.

Basically, REDA-LPP is an unsupervised feature extraction algorithm. In practice, we may extend it into a supervised version by setting $p_{ij}^t = 0$, if $c_i \neq c_j$. Interestingly, the supervised REDA-LPP also implies the robustness against outliers. It is known that at each iteration t, graph embedding problem (3.44) aims to preserve the sample pairwise similarity on the set $W^t X$ measured among the previous set $W^{t-1} X$. Typically, an outlier $W^{t-1} x_k$ is far away from the data cluster of its class and thus always receives low p_{kj}^t to $W^{t-1} x_j$ of the same class. Therefore, the outliers will have weaker influence on the estimation of W^t as t increases.

When $0 < \lambda \le 1$, the (3.43) in REDA is calculated as

$$W^t = \lambda \left(X(2(1-\lambda)L_p^t + \lambda LQ^t)X^T - \gamma I \right)^{-1} XLQ^t C^T. \tag{3.45}$$

- When $\lambda = 1$, by initializing $q_i^1 = -1$, the calculation of W^1 is equivalent to SRDA. When $t > 1$, the auxiliary variable $-q_i^t$ gives the weight of (x_i, c_i) for the estimation of W^t via SRDA. We refer to this version of our algorithm as REDA-SRDA, which is the solution of M-estimator (3.39).
- When $0 < \lambda < 1$, it is easy to see that, at each iteration t, (3.45) is the solution of a LapRLS problem with graph similarity matrix $-P^t$ based on previous representation. Such an iterative LapRLS feature extraction method reaps both the robustness of M-estimator and the advantage of manifold regularization. We call this version of our algorithm as REDA-LapRLS.

The connections of our REDA algorithm with existing algorithms are summarized in Table 3.1.

Table 3.1 Connections of REDA with existing algorithms [165]	Setting	Connections
	$\lambda = 0, \gamma = 0, t = 1$	Standard LPP [70]
	$\lambda = 0, \gamma = 0, t > 1$	Robust extension for LPP
	$\lambda = 1, t = 1$	Standard SRDA [15]
	$\lambda = 1, t > 1$	Robust extension for SRDA
	$\lambda \in (0,1), t = 1$	Standard LapRLS [8]
	$\lambda \in (0,1), t > 1$	Robust extension for LapRLS

3.2.2.5 Kernel Extension

Commonly, algorithm for linear feature extraction is computationally efficient for both projection matrix learning and final classification. However, its performance may degrade in cases with nonlinearly distributed data. A technique to extend methods for linear projections to nonlinear cases is to directly take advantage of the kernel trick. The intuition of the kernel trick is to map the data from the original input space to another higher dimensional Hilbert space as $\phi : X \mapsto Z$ and then perform the linear algorithm in this new feature space. This approach is well suited to algorithms that only need to compute the inner product of data pairs

$k(x_i,x_j) = \langle \phi(x_i), \phi(x_j) \rangle$. Assuming that the projection matrix $W = A\Phi$, where $\Phi = [\phi(x_1),\ldots,\phi(x_n)]^T$ and $\mathbf{K}$ is the kernel Gram matrix with entity $\mathbf{K}(i,j) = k(x_i,x_j)$, we have the following kernelization of problem (3.38):

$$A^* = \arg\max_A (1-\lambda) \sum_{i,j} g(A\mathbf{K}_i - A\mathbf{K}_j, \sqrt{2}\sigma)$$

$$+\lambda \sum_i l_i g(A\mathbf{K}_i - c_i, \sqrt{2}\sigma) - \gamma\|A\|_2,$$

where $\mathbf{K}_i$ indicates the ith column vector of the kernel Gram matrix $\mathbf{K}$. Accordingly, we can derive the so-called KREDA-LPP, KREDA-SRDA, and KREDA-LapRLS algorithms for robust kernel-based feature extraction.

3.2.2.6 Numerical Results on MNIST Database

In this section, we highlight some of the results in [165]. The MNIST handwritten digit database[2] is used to visualize the robustness of the proposed REDA-LPP, REDA-SRDA, and REDA-LapRLS. The MNIST database of handwritten digits has a training set A of 60,000 examples and a test set B of 10,000 examples. The digits have been size-normalized and centered in a fixed-size (28×28) bilevel image. We use the digits $\{3,8,9\}$ which represent difficult visual discrimination problem. We take the $\{3,8,9\}$ digits in the first 10,000 samples from set A as our training set and those in the first 10,000 from set B as our test set. A random subset with $n = (100,200,300)$ samples per digit from the training set is selected for training (with $m = 784$ and $n_c = 3$).

In this example, each digit class is of size $n = 300$ with $\eta = 50\%$ training samples being randomly mislabeled as the other digits. We set $\lambda = 0.99$ in REDA-LapRLS. When $t = 1$, the standard LPP (Fig. 3.4a), SRDA (Fig. 3.4c), and LapRLS (Fig. 3.4e) all perform poorly to discriminate classes in the learnt subspace due to mislabeling. When convergence is attained at $t = 6$ for all these three REDA algorithms, much more discriminative results are achieved, as can be seen in Fig. 3.4b, d, f.

3.3 Normalized Information Measures and Classification Evaluations

Evaluation measures, or metrics, have a substantial impact on the quality of classifications. The problem of how to select evaluation measures for the overall quality of classifications is difficult, and there appears no universal answer to this. While numerous performance measures have been applied in classification applications, this subsection focuses on *ITMs* for evaluations in abstaining classifications.

---

[2]http://yann.lecun.com/exdb/mnist/.

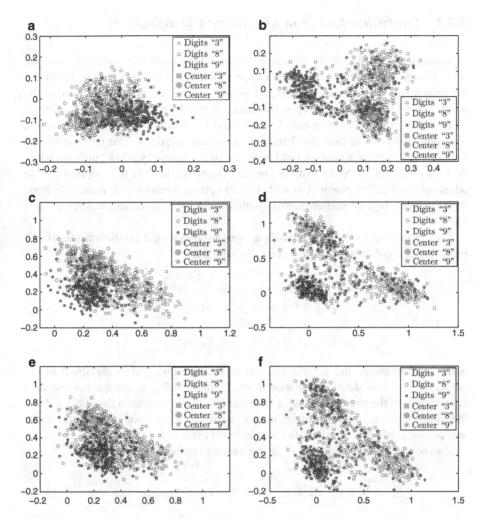

Fig. 3.4 Feature extraction results of a MNIST training set by REDA-LPP, REDA-SRDA, and REDA-LapRLS. Here, the first two dimensions of output features are plotted for visualization. Each class center is robustly estimated via iteratively reweighted least squares (IRLS) [165]. (**a**) REDA-LPP, $t = 1$; (**b**) REDA-LPP, $t = 6$; (**c**) REDA-SRDA, $t = 1$; (**d**) REDA-SRDA, $t = 6$; (**e**) REDA-LapRLS, $t = 1$; (**f**) REDA-LapRLS, $t = 6$

3.3.1 Confusion Matrix in Abstaining Classifications

Abstaining classifications are not a new concept in our daily life. Take, for example, a medical practice. A doctor may ask a patient to have medical exams. However, the total number of the exams is often depending on the decision confidence of the doctor. When the confidence is low, the doctor may ask more exams. For an extreme situation, a group of doctors may be requested for a joint decision. This example well demonstrates "abstention" behavior in human decisions. The purpose of this behavior is to reduce a cost (or risk) from a simple binary ("yes" or "no") decision. A third class, called "unknown" or "reject" class, is added in this application. To address classification evaluations with a reject option, we assume that the only basic data available is a confusion matrix, without any other information such as cost terms.

For abstaining multi-class classifications, an augmented confusion matrix, $\mathbf{C}$, including one column for a reject class, is defined by:

$$\mathbf{C} = \begin{bmatrix} c_{11} & c_{12} & \cdots & c_{1m} & c_{1(m+1)} \\ c_{21} & c_{22} & \cdots & c_{2m} & c_{2(m+1)} \\ & & \cdots & & \\ c_{m1} & c_{m2} & \cdots & c_{mm} & c_{m(m+1)} \end{bmatrix}, \tag{3.46}$$

where c_{ij} represents the sample number of the ith class that is classified as the jth class. The row data corresponds to the actual classes, while the column data corresponds to the predicted classes. The last column represents a reject class. Note that when a conventional confusion matrix is m-by-m for m class classifications, the augmented confusion matrix with a single reject class is m-by-$(m+1)$.

The relations and constraints of an augmented confusion matrix are:

$$C_i = \sum_{j=1}^{m+1} c_{ij}, \quad C_i > 0, \quad c_{ij} \geq 0, \quad i = 1, 2, \ldots, m, \tag{3.47}$$

where C_i is the total number for the ith class, which is generally known in classification problems.

For a binary classification, we can write the confusion matrix in a form of

$$\mathbf{C} = \begin{bmatrix} TN & FP & RN \\ FN & TP & RP \end{bmatrix}, \tag{3.48}$$

and

$$C_1 = TN + FP + RN, C_2 = FN + TP + RP, C_1 + C_2 = n, \tag{3.49}$$

where "TN," "TP," "FN," "FP," "RN," and "RP" represent "true negative," "true positive," "false negative," "false positive," "reject negative," and "reject positive," respectively. Following the conventions in binary classifications, we denote $FP(=c_{12})$ and $FN(=c_{21})$ by "Type I Error" and "Type II Error," respectively, and $RN(=c_{13})$ and $RP(=c_{23})$ by "Type I Reject" and "Type II Reject," respectively.

Conventional binary classifications usually distinguish two types of misclassification errors if they result in different losses in applications. For example, in a medical practice again, "Type I Error" (or FP) can be an error of misclassifying a healthy person to be abnormal, such as cancer. On the contrary, "Type II Error"(or FN) is an error where cancer is not detected in a patient. Therefore, "Type II Error" is more costly than "Type I Error." Based on the same reason for identifying "error types" in binary classifications, there is a need for considering "reject types" if a reject option is applied.

3.3.2 Meta-measures in Classification Evaluations

To select "proper" measures for evaluations in abstaining classifications, we propose the following three desirable features together with their heuristic reasons.

Feature 1. [75] Monotonicity with respect to the diagonal terms of the confusion matrix. The diagonal terms of the confusion matrix represent the exact classification numbers for all the samples. Or, they reflect the coincident numbers between the exact classes and the classified classes from a similarity viewpoint. When one of these terms changes, the evaluation measure should change in a monotonous way. Otherwise, any non-monotonic measure may fail to provide a rational result for ranking classifications correctly. This feature is proposed for describing the strength of agreement (or similarity) if the matrix is a contingency table [51].

Feature 2. [75] Variation with reject rate. A reject option in classifications is an important and effective strategy to reduce total cost. Therefore, we suggest that a measure should be a scalar function on both classification accuracy and reject rates. When a reject rate changes, the measure should be varied accordingly. Such a measure could be evaluated based solely on a given confusion matrix from a single operating point in the classification. This is different to the AUC measures that are calculated based on an "Error-Reject" curve from multiple operating points.

Feature 3. [75] Intuitively consistent costs among error types and reject types. This feature is derived from the principle of our conventional intuitions when dealing with error types in binary classifications. It is also extended to reject types. Two specific intuitions are adopted for binary classifications. First, a misclassification or rejection from a small class will cause a greater cost than that from a large class. This intuition represents a property called "within error types and reject types." Second, a misclassification will produce a greater cost than a rejection from the same class, which is called "between error and reject types" property. If a measure is able to satisfy the intuitions, we refer to its associated costs as being "intuitively consistent." Exceptions may exist to the intuitions above, but we consider them as a very special case.

Note that all desirable features above are derived from our intuitions on general cases of classification evaluations. Other items may be derived for a wider examination of features. For example, Forbes [51] proposed six "constraints on proper comparative measures." However, we consider the three features proposed above to be more crucial, especially as Feature 3 has never been concerned in previous studies of classification evaluations. Although Features 2 and 3 may share a similar meaning, they are presented individually to highlight their specific concerns.

We can also call the desirable features "meta-measures," because they are defined to be qualitative and high-level "measures about measures." We will apply meta-measures to examine each measure. We consider a measure "proper" if it satisfies the specific meta-measure. Otherwise, we call it "improper" to the given meta-measure. The examination with respect to the meta-measures enables clarification of the causes of performance differences among the examined measures in classification evaluations. It will be helpful for users to understand advantages and limitations of different measures, either performance or information ones, from a higher level of evaluation knowledge.

3.3.3   Normalized Information (NI) Measures

3.3.3.1   NI Based on Mutual Information

A normalized information measure, denoted as $NI(T,Y) \in [0,1]$, is a function based on information theory, which represents the degree of similarity between two random variables T and Y.

In principle, we hope that all NI measures satisfy the three important properties, or axioms, of metrics [92], supposing Z is another random variable:

P1: $NI(T,Y) = 1$ *iff* $T = Y$ (the identity axiom)
P2: $NI(T,Y) + NI(Y,Z) \geq NI(T,Z)$ (the triangle inequality)
P3: $NI(T,Y) = NI(Y,T)$ (the symmetry axiom)

Violations of properties of metrics are possible in reaching reasonable evaluations of classifications. For example, the triangle inequality and symmetry properties can be relaxed without changing the ranking orders among classifications if their evaluation measures are applied consistently. However, the identity property is indicated only for the relation $T = Y$ (assuming T is padded with a zero-value term to make it be the same size as Y) and does not guarantee an exact solution ($t_k = y_k$) in classifications (see Theorems 3.4 and 3.7 given later). Because a violation of metric properties may occur to NI, we refer it as a "measure," rather than a "metric."

All information measures studied here are divided into one of three groups, namely, mutual-information-based, divergence-based, and cross-entropy-based groups. In this subsection, we focus on the first group. Each measure in this group is derived directly from mutual information for representing the degree of similarity between two random variables. For the purpose of objective evaluations without any influence from free parameters, we eliminate all candidate measures defined from the Renyi or Jensen entropies since they involve a free parameter. Therefore, we only apply the Shannon entropy to information measures [31]:

$$H(Y) = -\sum_y p(y)\log_2 p(y), \tag{3.50}$$

where Y is a discrete random variable with probability mass function $p(y)$. Then mutual information is defined as [31]

$$I(T,Y) = \sum_t \sum_y p(t,y)\log_2 \frac{p(t,y)}{p(t)p(y)}, \tag{3.51}$$

where $p(t,y)$ is the joint distribution for the two discrete random variables T and Y and $p(t)$ and $p(y)$ are called marginal distributions that can be derived from

$$p(t) = \sum_y p(t,y), p(y) = \sum_t p(t,y). \tag{3.52}$$

Sometimes, the simplified notations for $p_{ij} = p(t,y) = p(t=t_i, y=y_j)$ are used in this work. Table 3.2 lists the possible normalized information measures ($NI_k, k = 1,2,\ldots,9$) within the mutual-information-based group. Basically, they all make use of (3.50) in their calculations. The main differences are due to the normalization schemes. In applying the formulas for calculating NI_k, one generally does not have an exact $p(t,y)$. For this reason, we adopt an empirical joint distribution defined below for the calculations.

An empirical joint distribution is defined from the frequency means for the given confusion matrix, $\mathbf{C}$, as [76]

$$P_e(t,y) = (P_{ij})_e = \frac{1}{n}c_{ij}, \ i = 1,\ldots,m, \ j = 1,\ldots,m+1, \tag{3.53}$$

where $n = \sum C_i$ denotes the total number of samples in the classifications. The subscript "e" is given for denoting empirical terms. The empirical marginal distributions are:

$$P_e(t=t_i) = \frac{C_i}{n}, \quad i = 1,2,\ldots,m. \tag{3.54}$$

$$P_e(y=y_j) = \frac{1}{n}\sum_{i=1}^m c_{ij}, \quad j = 1,2,\ldots,m+1. \tag{3.55}$$

The empirical mutual information is given by [76]

$$I_e(T,Y) = \sum_t \sum_y P_e(t,y) \log_2 \frac{P_e(t,y)}{P_e(t)P_e(y)}$$

$$= \sum_{i=1}^{m} \sum_{j=1}^{m+1} \frac{c_{ij}}{n} \log_2 \left(\frac{c_{ij}}{C_i \sum_{i=1}^{m} \frac{c_{ij}}{n}} \right) sgn(c_{ij}), \qquad (3.56)$$

where $sgn(.)$ is a sign function for satisfying the definition of $H(0) = 0$. For the sake of simplicity of expressions, we hereafter neglect the sign function.

Definitions above provide users with a direct means for applying information measures through the given data of the confusion matrix. For the sake of simplicity of analysis and discussion, we adopt the empirical distributions, or $p_{ij} \approx P_{ij}$, for calculating all NIs and deriving the following three theorems, but removing their associated subscript "e."

Theorem 3.4 ([75]). *Within all NI measures in Table 3.2, when $NI(T,Y) = 1$, the classification without a reject class may correspond to the case of either an exact classification ($y_k = t_k$) or a specific misclassification ($y_k \neq t_k$). The specific misclassification can be fully removed by simply exchanging labels in the confusion matrix.*

Proof. If $NI(T,Y) = 1$, we can obtain the following conditions from (3.56) for classifications without a reject class:

$$p_{ij} = p(t = t_i) \approx P_e(t = t_i) = \frac{C_i}{n} \qquad (3.57)$$

and

$$p_{kj} = 0, \quad i,j,k = 1,2,\ldots,m, \quad k \neq i. \qquad (3.58)$$

These conditions describe the specific confusion matrix where only one nonzero term appears in each column (with the exception of the last $(m + 1)$th column). When $j = i$, **C** is a diagonal matrix for representing an exact classification ($y_k = t_k$). Otherwise, a specific misclassification exists for which a diagonal matrix can be obtained by exchanging labels in the confusion matrix. □

Theorem 3.4 describes that NI(T,Y)=1 presents a necessary, but not sufficient, condition of an exact classification.

Theorem 3.5 ([75]). *For abstaining classification problems, when $NI(T,Y) = 0$, the classifier generally reflects a misclassification. One special case is that all samples are considered to be one of m classes, or be a reject class.*

Proof. For NIs defined in Table 3.2, $NI(T,Y) = 0$ *iff* $I(T,Y) = 0$. According to information theory [31], the following conditions can hold based on the given marginal distributions (or the empirical ones if a confusion matrix is used):

$$I(T,Y) = 0, \quad iff \quad p(t,y) = p(t)p(y). \tag{3.59}$$

The conditional part in (3.59) can be rewritten in the form $p_{ij} = p(t = t_i)p(y = y_j)$. From the constraints in (3.47), $p(t = t_i) > 0 \ (i = 1,2,\ldots,m)$ can be obtained. For classification solutions, there should exist at least one term for $p(y = y_j) > 0 \ (j = 1,2,\ldots,m+1)$. Therefore, at least one nonzero term for $p_{ij} > 0 \ (i \neq j)$ must be obtained. This nonzero term corresponds to the off-diagonal term in the confusion matrix, which indicates that a misclassification has occurred. When all samples have been identified as one of the classes, $NI = 0$ should be obtained. □

Equation (3.59) gives the statistical reason for zero mutual information, that is, the two random variables are "statistically independent." Theorem 3.5 demonstrates an intrinsic reason for local minima in NIs.

Theorem 3.6 ([75]). *The NI measures defined by the Shannon entropy generally do not exhibit a monotonic property with respect to the diagonal terms of a confusion matrix.*

Proof. Based on [76], we arrive at simpler conditions for the local minima about $I(T,Y)$ for the given confusion matrix:

$$C = \begin{bmatrix} \cdots & 0 & 0 & \cdots \\ 0 & c_{i,i} & c_{i,i+1} & 0 \\ 0 & c_{i+1,i} & c_{i+1,i+1} & 0 \\ \cdots & 0 & 0 & \cdots \end{bmatrix}, \ if \ \frac{c_{i,i}}{c_{i+1,i}} = \frac{c_{i,i+1}}{c_{i+1,i+1}}. \tag{3.60}$$

The local minima are obtained because the four given nonzero terms in (3.60) produce zero (or the minimum) contribution to $I(T,Y)$. Suppose a generic form is given for $NI(T,Y) = g(I(T,Y))$, where $g(\cdot)$ is a normalization function. From the chain rule of derivatives, it can be seen that the conditions do not change for reaching the local minima. □

The non-monotonic property of the information measures implies that these measures may suffer from an intrinsic problem of local minima for classification rankings. Or, according to Feature 1 of the meta-measures, a rational result for the classification evaluations may not be obtained due to the non-monotonic property of the measures.

Note that the notation of NI_2 in Table 3.2 differs from the others for calculating mutual information, where $I_M(T,Y)$ is defined as "modified mutual information." The calculation of $I_M(T,Y)$ is carried out based on the intersection of T and Y. Hence, when using (3.56), the intersection requires that $I_M(T,Y)$ incorporates a summation of j over 1 to m, instead of $m + 1$. This definition is beyond

Table 3.2 NI measures within the mutual-information-based group [75]

No.	Name	Formula on NI_k
1	NI based on mutual information	$NI_1(T,Y) = \frac{I(T,Y)}{H(T)}$
2	NI based on mutual information	$NI_2(T,Y) = \frac{I_M(T,Y)}{H(T)}$
3	NI based on mutual information	$NI_3(T,Y) = \frac{I(T,Y)}{H(Y)}$
4	NI based on mutual information	$NI_4(T,Y) = \frac{1}{2}\left[\frac{I(T,Y)}{H(T)} + \frac{I(T,Y)}{H(Y)}\right]$
5	NI based on mutual information	$NI_5(T,Y) = \frac{2I(T,Y)}{H(T)+H(Y)}$
6	NI based on mutual information	$NI_6(T,Y) = \frac{I(T,Y)}{\sqrt{H(T)H(Y)}}$
7	NI based on mutual information	$NI_7(T,Y) = \frac{I(T,Y)}{H(T,Y)}$
8	NI based on mutual information	$NI_8(T,Y) = \frac{I(T,Y)}{\max(H(T),H(Y))}$
9	NI based on mutual information	$NI_9(T,Y) = \frac{I(T,Y)}{\min(H(T),H(Y))}$

mathematical rigor. It was originally proposed to overcome the problem of unchanging values in NIs if rejections are made within only one class. More discussions about this measure are given on Sect. 3.3.3.4.

3.3.3.2 NI Based on Information Divergence

In this subsection, we propose normalized information measures based on the definition of information divergence. Table 3.3 lists the commonly used divergence measures, which are denoted as $D_k(T,Y)$, and represent dissimilarity between the two random variables T and Y. We apply the following notations for defining marginal distributions:

$$p_t(z) = p_t(t = z) = p(t), \text{ and } p_y(z) = p_y(y = z) = p(y), \tag{3.61}$$

where z is a possible scalar value that t or y can take. For a consistent comparison with the previous normalized information measures, we adopt the following transformation on D_k [113]:

$$NI_k = \exp(-D_k). \tag{3.62}$$

This transformation provides both inverse and normalization functionalities. It does not introduce any extra parameters and presents a high degree of simplicity, as in derivation for examining the local minima. Two more theorems are derived by following a similar analysis to that in the previous subsection.

Theorem 3.7 ([75]). *For all NI measures in Table 3.3, when $NI(T,Y) = 1$, the classifier corresponds to the case of either an exact classification or a specific misclassification. Generally, the misclassification in the latter case cannot be removed by switching labels in the confusion matrix.*

Proof. When $p_y(z) = p_t(z)$, it is always the case that $NI(T,Y) = 1$. However, general conditions can be given for $p_y(z) = p_t(z)$ as follows:

$$p_y(y = z_i) = p_t(t = z_i),$$

$$or \sum_j P_{ji} = \sum_j p_{ij}, \quad i = 1, 2, \ldots, m \tag{3.63}$$

Equation (3.63) implies two cases of classifications for $D_k(T,Y) = 0, (k = 10, \ldots, 20)$. One of these corresponds to an exact classification (or $y_k = t_k$), while the other is the result of a specific misclassification that shows the relationship of $y_k \neq t_k$, but $p_y(z) = p_t(z)$. In the latter case, switching labels in the confusion matrix to remove misclassification generally destroys the relation for $p_y(z) = p_t(z)$ at the same time. Considering the relation is a necessary condition for a perfect classification, the misclassification cannot be removed through a label switching operation. □

Theorem 3.7 suggests the caution should be applied in explaining the classification evaluations when $NI(T,Y) = 1$. The maximum of the NIs from the information divergence measures only indicates the equivalence between the marginal probabilities, $p_y(z) = p_t(z)$, but this is not always true for representing exact classifications (or $y_k = t_k$). Theorem 3.7 reveals an intrinsic problem when using an NI as a measure for similarity evaluations between two datasets, such as in image registration.

Theorem 3.8 ([75]). *The NI measures based on information divergence generally do not exhibit a monotonic property with respect to the diagonal terms of confusion matrix.*

Proof. The theorem can be proved by examining the existence of multiple maxima for NI measures based on information divergence. Here we use a binary classification as an example. The local minima of D_k are obtained when the following conditions exist for a confusion matrix:

$$\mathbf{C} = \begin{bmatrix} C_1 - d_1 & d_1 & 0 \\ d_2 & C_2 - d_2 & 0 \end{bmatrix} \quad and \quad d_1 = d_2, \tag{3.64}$$

where d_1 and d_2 are integer numbers (> 0) for misclassified samples. The confusion matrix in (3.64) produces zero divergence D_k and therefore, $NI_k = 1$. However, changing from $d_1 \neq d_2$ always results in $NI_k < 1$. The problem above can extend to the general classifications in (3.46). □

Theorem 3.8 indicates another shortcoming of NIs in the information divergence group from the viewpoint of monotonicity. The reason is once again attributed to the usage of marginal distributions in calculations of divergence. The shortcoming has not been reported in previous investigations [92, 113].

Table 3.3 Information measures within the divergence-based group [75]

No.	Name of D_k	Formula on D_k $(NI_k = exp(-D_k))$
10	ED-quadratic divergence	$D_{10} = QD_{ED}(T,Y) = \sum_z (p_t(z) - p_y(z))^2$
11	CS-quadratic divergence	$D_{11} = QD_{CS}(T,Y) = \log_2 \frac{\sum_z p_t(z)^2 \sum_z p_y(z)^2}{[\sum_z (p_t(z)p_y(z))]^2}$
12	KL divergence	$D_{12} = KL(T,Y) = \sum_z p_t(z) \log_2 \frac{p_t(z)}{p_y(z)}$
13	Bhattacharyya distance	$D_{13} = D_B(T,Y) = -\log_2 \sum_z \sqrt{p_t(z)p_y(z)}$
14	χ^2 (Pearson) divergence	$D_{14} = \chi^2(T,Y) = \sum_z \frac{(p_t(z)-p_y(z))^2}{p_y(z)}$
15	Hellinger distance	$D_{15} = H^2(T,Y) = \sum_z (\sqrt{p_t(z)} - \sqrt{p_y(z)})^2$
16	Variation distance	$D_{16} = V(T,Y) = \sum_z |p_t(z) - p_y(z)|$
17	J divergence	$D_{17} = J(T,Y) = \sum_z p_t(z) \log_2 \frac{p_t(z)}{p_y(z)} + \sum_z p_y(z) \log_2 \frac{p_y(z)}{p_t(z)}$
18	L (or JS) divergence	$D_{18} = L(T,Y) = KL(T,M) + KL(Y,M), M = \frac{(p_t(z)+p_y(z))}{2}$
19	Symmetric χ^2 divergence	$D_{19} = \chi_S^2(T,Y) = \sum_z \frac{(p_t(z)-p_y(z))^2}{p_y(z)} + \sum_z \frac{(p_y(z)-p_t(z))^2}{p_t(z)}$
20	Resistor average distance	$D_{20} = D_{RA}(T,Y) = \frac{KL(T,Y)KL(Y,T)}{KL(T,Y)+KL(Y,T)}$

3.3.3.3   NI Based on Cross-Entropy

In this subsection, we propose normalized information measures based on cross-entropy, which is defined for discrete random variables as

$$H(T;Y) = -\sum_z p_t(z) \log_2 p_y(z), \tag{3.65}$$

or

$$H(Y;T) = -\sum_z p_y(z) \log_2 p_t(z). \tag{3.66}$$

Note that $H(T;Y)$ differs from joint-entropy $H(T,Y)$ with respect to both notation and definition and is given as [31]

$$H(T,Y) = -\sum_t \sum_y p(t,y) \log_2 p(t,y). \tag{3.67}$$

In fact, from (3.66), one can derive the relation between KL divergence (see Table 3.3) and cross-entropy:

$$H(T;Y) = H(T) + KL(T,Y),$$
$$or \quad H(Y;T) = H(Y) + KL(Y,T). \tag{3.68}$$

Table 3.4 NI measures within the cross-entropy-based group [75]

No.	Name	Formula on NI_k
21	NI based on cross-entropy	$NI_{21} = \frac{H(T)}{H(T;Y)}, H(T;Y) = -\sum_z p_t(z)\log_2 p_y(z)$
22	NI based on cross-entropy	$NI_{22} = \frac{H(Y)}{H(Y;T)}, H(Y;T) = -\sum_z p_y(z)\log_2 p_t(z)$
23	NI based on cross-entropy	$NI_{23} = \frac{1}{2}\left(\frac{H(T)}{H(T;Y)} + \frac{H(Y)}{H(Y;T)}\right)$
24	NI based on cross-entropy	$NI_{24} = \frac{H(T)+H(Y)}{H(T;Y)+H(Y;T)}$

If $H(T)$ is considered as a constant in classification since the target dataset is generally known and fixed, we can observe from (3.3.3.3) that cross-entropy shares a similar meaning as KL divergence for representing dissimilarity between T and Y. From the conditions $H \geq 0$ and $KL \geq 0$, we are able to realize the normalization for cross-entropy shown in Table 3.4. Following similar discussions as in the previous subsection, we can derive that all information measures listed in Table 3.4 will also satisfy Theorems 3.7 and 3.8 respectively.

3.3.3.4 Discussions on NI_2 Measure

Among all the measures concerned, only NI_2 in Table 3.5 shows the "best" solutions to the numerical examples in abstaining classifications [75], particularly its uniqueness in terms of Feature 3. For knowing this measure well, we highlight the discussion in [75] specifically in this subsection.

Table 3.5 Comparisons of evaluation measures related to the meta-measures (Yes = satisfied, No = not satisfied)

Measure(s)	Feature 1	Feature 2	Feature 3
$A, E, CR, F1, AUC, Precision$	Yes	No	No
$Recall$	No	No	No
Rej	No	Yes	No
$NI_1, NI_3\text{-}NI_{24}$	No	Yes	No
NI_2	No	Yes	Yes

Theorem 3.9. *In regard to the meta-measure of Feature 2, the conventional mutual information $I(t,y)$ is improper, but the modified mutual information $I_M(t,y)$ is proper.*

Proof. For a given **C**, where $c_{k(m+1)} > 0$ and $c_{i(m+1)} = 0$, $(i = 1,2,\ldots,m,$ but $i \neq k)$, one can show that its $I(t,y)$ will be unchanged for any change of $c_{k(m+1)}$. This special setting is simple and sufficient as a counterexample to confirm that $I(t,y)$ is improper in terms of Feature 2. Next is a proof on $I_M(t,y)$. Suppose for a given **C**, only reject rates change in a way $c_{k(m+1)} + \Delta_k$, where Δ_k is the change in the kth class. Mutual information holds a summation property, that is, each element of $\mathbf{C}$ has a contribution to the total mutual information by a summation way. $I_M(t,y)$ does not take the elements from the last column of $\mathbf{C}$ into account for mutual information contribution. Therefore, only diagonal elements $c_{kk} - \Delta_k$ will determine the changes of $I_M(t,y)$. The continuity of $I_M(t,y)$ with respect to Δ_k will ensure the changes of $I_M(t,y)$ whenever $\Delta_k \neq 0$. $\square$

Numerical examples are given for understanding Theorem 3.9. Giving two matrices,

$$\mathbf{C}_A = \begin{bmatrix} 90 & 0 & 0 \\ 0 & 9 & 1 \end{bmatrix}, \quad \mathbf{C}_B = \begin{bmatrix} 88 & 0 & 2 \\ 0 & 10 & 0 \end{bmatrix},$$

the solutions from NI_1 and NI_2 are:

$$NI_1(\mathbf{C}_A) = 1.0, \quad NI_1(\mathbf{C}_B) = 1.0,$$

$$NI_2(\mathbf{C}_A) = 0.929, \quad NI_2(\mathbf{C}_B) = 0.994.$$

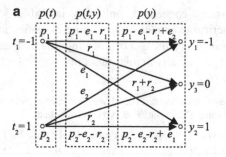

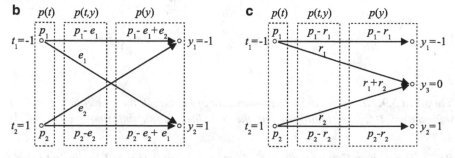

Fig. 3.5 Abstaining binary classifications [(**a**) general binary channel (GBC), (**b**) binary asymmetric channel (BAC), (**c**) binary asymmetric erasure channel (BAEC)] from a perspective of information coding. (**b**) and (**c**) are modified based on [104]

The examples above suggest an important finding even from a perspective of information coding. In coding applications, a *binary symmetric channel* (BSC) and a *binary erasure channel* (BEC) are basic and common models [31]. Recently, their asymmetric versions, namely a *binary asymmetric channel* (BAC) and a *binary asymmetric erasure channel* (BAEC), are getting attentions [104]. In Fig. 3.5a, we can term an abstaining binary classification to be a *general binary channel* (GBC). Figure 3.5 shows GBC, BAC, and BAEC channels, respectively. They are modified based on [104]. Different from the conventional notations [31, 104] using *conditional probability* (or *transition matrix*) $p(y|t)$, we apply *joint probability distributions* $p(t,y)$ to describe the channels. Theorem 3.9 suggests an issue which seems to be overlooked in the existing studies.

Theorem 3.10 ([75]). *For a binary classification, NI_2 satisfies Feature 3 on the property regarding error types and reject types around the exact classifications. Specifically for the four confusion matrices below:*

$$C_1 = \begin{bmatrix} C_1 & 0 & 0 \\ d & C_2 - d & 0 \end{bmatrix}, \ C_2 = \begin{bmatrix} C_1 - d & d & 0 \\ 0 & C_2 & 0 \end{bmatrix},$$

$$C_3 = \begin{bmatrix} C_1 & 0 & 0 \\ 0 & C_2 - d & d \end{bmatrix}, \ C_4 = \begin{bmatrix} C_1 - d & 0 & d \\ 0 & C_2 & 0 \end{bmatrix},$$

$$for \ \ C_1 > C_2 > d > 0,$$

the following relations will be held:

$$NI_2(C_4) > NI_2(C_3) > NI_2(C_2) > NI_2(C_1)$$

$$for \ \ 0.5 < p_1 < p_c \le 1$$

$$NI_2(C_4) > NI_2(C_2) > NI_2(C_3) > NI_2(C_1)$$

$$for \ \ 0.5 < p_c < p_1 \le 1$$

where p_c is a critical boundary and $p_1 = C_1/n$.

The proof is quite tedious and one can refer to the detailed derivations in [75]. A closed-form study is made to information cost on the basis of an exact classification:

$$C_0 = \begin{bmatrix} C_1 & 0 & 0 \\ 0 & C_2 & 0 \end{bmatrix}.$$

The information cost is denoted by $|\Delta I|$ where ΔI is mutual information difference between the two matrices, such as,

$$\Delta I_{10} = I_M(C_1) - I_M(C_0), \ \Delta I_{20} = I_M(C_2) - I_M(C_0),$$

$$\Delta I_{30} = I_M(C_3) - I_M(C_0), \ \Delta I_{40} = I_M(C_4) - I_M(C_0).$$

Figure 3.6 depicts the plots of "ΔI vs. p_1" when $d = 1$ and $n = 100$, which shows a better interoperation to Theorem 3.10. When the classes are balanced, $p_1 = p_2 = 0.5$, the plots indicate that $\mathbf{C}_3$ and $\mathbf{C}_4$ share the same information cost which is smaller than that from $\mathbf{C}_1$ and $\mathbf{C}_2$. When $p_1 > 0.5$, the four plots verify that NI_2 measures satisfy Feature 3 in terms of information cost. The plots of ΔI_{20} and ΔI_{30} reveal a novel finding about "Which costs more, a misclassification from a large class or a rejection from a small class?" The finding confirms that information theory is principally general to deal with errors, rejects, and their relations.

Fig. 3.6 Plots of "ΔI vs. p_1" when $n = 100$, $d = 1$ and $p_c \approx 0.94$ [75]

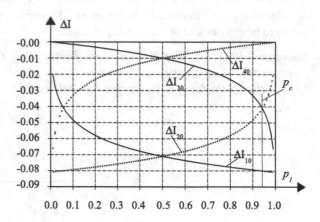

3.4 Summary

In this chapter, different information-theoretic measures have been studied for data understanding and abstaining classifications. We presented unsupervised and supervised subspace learning methods based on Shannon entropy and Renyi's quadratic entropy, and examined how these methods are able to visualize hidden structure of high-dimensional data. These methods combine the main benefits of information-theoretic measures and traditional subspace learning. As a result, they can learn a robust low-dimensional representation of the data, in which both the structure and metric of the data are preserved. In addition, we also discuss how to select information theoretic measures to evaluate the overall quality of classifications. A reject option is considered in classifications, which provides an alternative means of achieving robust recognition. Developing new information theoretic measures [130] and applying existing measures to real-world problems (such as big data) are always hot issues in machine learning. Developing or selecting an appropriate information measure may facilitate problem solving.

Chapter 4
Correntropy and Linear Representation

The nearest neighbor (NN) classifier is the most popular method for image-based object recognition. In NN classifier, the representational capacity of an image database and the recognition rate depend on how registered samples are selected to represent object's possible variations and also how many samples are available. However, in practice, only a small number of samples are available for an object class. Hence linear representation methods are developed to generalize the representational capacity of available samples.

Since linear representation methods are often sensitive to outliers, robust estimation is often used to improve robustness. One commonly used robust estimation for linear representation is correntropy [99]. Hence, in this chapter, we firstly describe the fundamental theories and properties of correntropy. And then we present linear representation and robust linear representation methods for image-based object recognition. In particular, we show that ℓ_2 regularized correntropy has a better stability in linear representation methods.

4.1 Correntropy

Correntropy is an important concept in information theoretic learning [99]. The name correntropy comes from correlation and entropy. It is derived from Renyi's quadratic entropy and has a close relationship to M-estimation in the sense of Welsch M-estimator [99]. It can be used for robust M-estimation [99] or an approximator of ℓ_0-norm in sparse estimation [136].

Correntropy is defined as a generalized similarity measure between two arbitrary random variables A and B [99]:

$$V_\sigma(A, B) = E[k_\sigma(A, B)], \tag{4.1}$$

© The Author(s) 2014
R. He et al., *Robust Recognition via Information Theoretic Learning*,
SpringerBriefs in Computer Science, DOI 10.1007/978-3-319-07416-0_4

where $k_\sigma(.)$ is the kernel function that satisfies Mercer's theory [146] and $E[.]$ denotes the mathematical expectation. It takes advantage of the kernel technique that nonlinearly maps the input space to a higher dimensional space. It has a clear theoretical foundation and is symmetric, positive, and bounded.

In practice, the joint probability density function is often unknown and only a finite number of data $\{(a_i, b_i)\}_{i=1}^n$ are available, which lead to the following sample estimator of correntropy:

$$\hat{V}_{d,\sigma}(A, B) = \frac{1}{n} \sum_{i=1}^n k_\sigma(a_i, b_i). \tag{4.2}$$

When k_σ is the Gaussian kernel function $k_\sigma(a_i, b_i) \triangleq g(a_i - b_i) = \exp(-\frac{(a_i - b_i)^2}{2\sigma^2})$, we can rewrite (4.2) as

$$\hat{V}_{d,\sigma}(A, B) = \frac{1}{n} \sum_{i=1}^n g(a_i - b_i). \tag{4.3}$$

The maximum of correntropy of error in (4.2) is called the maximum correntropy criterion (MCC) [99].

Compared with the global measure—mean square error (MSE)—MCC is local along the bisector of the joint space and lies on the first quadrant of a sphere, which means that the value of correntropy is mainly decided by the kernel function along the line $A = B$ [99]. Correntropy has a close relationship with redescending M-estimators [77]. Reference [99] firstly imposed it and proved that correntropy is a robust function (in the sense of Huber) for linear and nonlinear regression. A main merit of correntropy is that the kernel size controls all the properties of correntropy [99]. It provides a practical way to choose an appropriate kernel size [99].

4.1.1 Properties of Correntropy

Some important properties of correntropy [99, 135] are presented here. These properties are presented in [99, 135] and will, therefore, not be proved here.

Property 4.1 ([135]). Correntropy is symmetric: $V_\sigma(A, B) = V_\sigma(B, A)$.

Property 4.2 ([135]). Correntropy is positive and bounded: $0 < V(A, B) \leq 1/(\sqrt{2\pi}\sigma)$. It reaches its maximum if and only if $A = B$.

Property 4.3 ([135]). Correntropy involves all the even moments of the random variable $E = B - A$: $V_\sigma(A, B) = 1/(\sqrt{2\pi}\sigma) \sum_{m=0}^\infty ((-1)^m)/(2^m m!) E\left[(A - B)^{2m}/\sigma^{2m}\right]$.

These three properties demonstrate that correntropy is symmetric, positive, and bounded. Since the high-order moments decay faster as σ increases, the second-order moment tends to dominate correntropy and makes correntropy approach correlation. Due to the expected value operator, the issue of kernel size selection of σ is different from density estimation. And the performance sensitivity of correntropy to σ is much less than what could be expected from density estimation [99].

Property 4.4 ([99]). Assume data $\{(a_i, b_i)\}_{i=1}^{n}$ are drawn from the joint PDF $f_{A,B}(a,b)$, and $\hat{f}_{A,B;\sigma}(a,b)$ is Parzen estimate with kernel size σ. The correntropy estimate with kernel size $\sigma' = \sqrt{2}\sigma$ is the integral of $\hat{f}_{A,B;\sigma}(a,b)$ along the line $a = b$:

$$\hat{V}_{\sqrt{2}\sigma} = \int_{-\infty}^{+\infty} \hat{f}_{A,B;\sigma}(a,b)|_{a=b=u}\,du$$

In practical applications, correntropy is estimated only with a finite number of samples, which sets a lower bound on the kernel size. When the kernel size used in correntropy is σ, its rectangle approximation has a bandwidth $\sqrt{\pi/2}\sigma$ [99].

4.1.2 Correntropy Minimization

The major difficulty of the minimization of correntropy is that they involve the Gaussian kernel function. Many methods, such as Newton gradient and Taylor expansion [59], can be used to minimize these entropy induced loss functions. Since this Gaussian function is related to Welsch M-estimator [99], it can be approximately minimized by half-quadratic optimization. In this subsection, we highlight some theoretic results in [159] to minimize correntropy.

Suppose that we have a kernel function $\phi(.)$ satisfying:

(1) $\phi(x)$ is convex on R^+,
(2) $\phi(x)$ is monotonically decreasing and C^1 is continuous on R^+,
(3) $\phi(x)$ is bounded on R^+,
(4) $\phi'(x)$ is bounded on R^+,

then, we have the following theorem.

Theorem 4.1 ([159]). *Let $\phi(.)$ be a kernel satisfying all above conditions, then there exists a convex function $\varphi : R \rightarrow R$, such that*

$$\phi(x) = \sup_{p \subset R^-} (px - \varphi(p))$$

Proof. The proof is based on the theory of convex conjugated functions [13, 131], which tells that given a function $f : R \rightarrow R$, its conjugated function g is defined by $g(p) = \sup_{x \in R}\{px - f(x)\}$ and is convex on R. If f is continuous and convex, we have reciprocally $f(x) = \sup_{p \in R}\{px - g(p)\}$. Define $\theta : R \rightarrow R$ as

$$\theta(x) = \begin{cases} \phi(x), x > 0 \\ +\infty \;\; x \leq 0 \end{cases} \tag{4.4}$$

According to the definition of θ, the function θ is convex on R. The conjugate function of θ takes the form

$$\varphi(p) = \sup_{x \in R^+} \{q(x,p)\}, \tag{4.5}$$

where $q(x,p) = px - \theta(x)$. From the abovementioned theory of convex conjugated functions, we have $\varphi(p)$ is convex, which results in

$$\theta(x) = \sup_{p \in R^-} \{px - \varphi(p)\}, \tag{4.6}$$

where the supremum is taken over R^- because $\varphi(p) = +\infty$ if $p > 0$, according to condition (4.6). Since $\theta(x)$ is convex, we have that for any $p < 0$, the function $x \to q(x,p)$ is concave on R^+ and satisfies $\lim_{x \to \infty} q(x,p) = -\infty$. It follows that $q(x,p)$ reaches its supremum at a finite $x \in R^+$. For a fixed-point p^*, the supremum of (4.5) is reached at a finite $x^* > 0$ so that $p^* = \theta'(x^*) = \phi'(x^*)$. By duality, for any x, we obtain that the supremum of (4.6) is reached at $p = \phi'(x) < 0$. By restricting $\theta(x)$ on R^+, we have this theorem. $\square$

Theorem 4.2 ([159]). *There exists a convex function* $\varphi : R \to R$, *such that*

$$exp(-x^2/\sigma^2) = \sup_{p \in R^-} (p\frac{x^2}{\sigma^2} - \varphi(p)),$$

and for a fixed x, the supremum is reached at $p = -exp(-x^2/\sigma^2)$.

Proof. According to Theorem 4.1, let $\phi(x) = exp(-x)$ and replace x with x^2/σ^2; we have this theorem. $\square$

Based on Theorem 4.2, we can solve a correntropy induced loss function in a half-quadratic way. When the auxiliary variable p is fixed, complex entropy problems can be simplified to a quadratic problem. In the following chapters, we will further introduce regularized correntropy techniques for robust recognition.

4.2 Correntropy Induced Metric (CIM)

Correntropy, as a sample estimator, induces a metric in the sample space. Given two vectors $A = (a_1, a_2, \ldots, a_n)$ and $B = (b_1, b_2, \ldots, b_n)$ in the sample space, the function

$$CIM(A,B) = (k_\sigma(0) - V(A,B))^{1/2} \tag{4.7}$$

defines a metric in the sample space and is named as the correntropy induced metric (CIM) [99]. CIM satisfies the following properties [99]:

(1) Nonnegativity—$CIM(A,B) \geq 0$
(2) Identity of indiscernibles—$CIM(A,B) = 0$ if and only if $A = B$
(3) Symmetric—$CIM(A,B) = CIM(B,A)$
(4) Triangle inequality—$CIM(A,Z) \leq CIM(A,B) + CIM(B,Z)$

CIM is also translation invariant for translation-invariant kernels like the Gaussian kernel, so $V(A,B)$ can be denoted as $V(B-A)$. However, CIM is not homogenous so that it does not induce a norm on the sample space [99].

4.2.1 CIM and ℓ_0-Norm

In compressed sensing, ℓ_0-norm is defined as the number of nonzero entries in the vector A, i.e., $\|A\|_0$. Minimizing ℓ_0-norm is an NP hard problem due to a non-continuous property [39]. Hence, ℓ_0-norm is often approximated by continuous functions. A popular approximation is as follows:

$$\|A\|_0 \sim \sum_{i=1}^{N} \{1 - \exp(-c|a_i|)\}, \tag{4.8}$$

where c is a positive constant. For practical purposes, c can be increased slowly during optimization for a better approximation. Another approximator is given by

$$\|A\|_0 \sim \sum_{i=1}^{N} \log(|a_i| + c). \tag{4.9}$$

Seth and Principe [136] show that CIM can be used as an approximation of ℓ_0-norm, i.e.,

$$\|A\|_0 \sim CIM(A,0) = \sqrt{1 - \frac{1}{n}\sum_{i=1}^{n} k(a_i,0)} = \sqrt{\frac{1}{n}\sum_{i=1}^{n}(1 - \exp(\frac{a_i^2}{2\sigma^2}))}, \tag{4.10}$$

where $k(a,b)$ is a Gaussian kernel. We can also simplify (4.10) by removing the square root operator. Hence (4.10) takes the form

$$\|A\|_0 \sim CIM^2(A,0) = \frac{1}{n}\sum_{i=1}^{n}(1 - \exp(\frac{a_i^2}{2\sigma^2})). \tag{4.11}$$

Gaussian kernel-based CIM changes from an ℓ_2 metric to ℓ_1 and finally to ℓ_0 depending upon the distance between the samples. And this flexibility can be used as an approximator of ℓ_0-norm in compressive sampling [136]. Figure 4.1 shows the curves of different approximators of ℓ_0-norm. Theoretical analysis in [136] shows that CIM as an approximator of ℓ_0-norm performs better than both ℓ_1-norm and $\ell_{0.75}$-norm in terms of required number of measurements.

Since the definition of CIM does not restrict the kernel $k(.)$ to Gaussian kernel, a Laplacian kernel $k(a,b) = (c/2)exp(-c|a-b|)$ is another possible kernel. If we use Laplacian kernel in CIM, then the approximation of ℓ_0-norm takes the form of (4.8).

Fig. 4.1 Different approximators of ℓ_0-norm. Correntropy induced metric changes from an ℓ_2 metric to ℓ_1 and finally to ℓ_0 depending upon the bandwidth in its Gaussian kernel

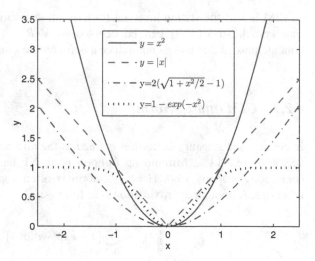

4.2.2   CIM and M-Estimation

In the case of adaptive systems, θ is a set of adjustable parameters and e is an error produced by the system during learning. We consider the following correntropy minimization problem:

$$\min_{\theta} CIM^2(e|\theta,0). \tag{4.12}$$

When Gaussian kernel is used, (4.12) takes the form

$$\min_{\theta} CIM^2(e|\theta,0) = \min_{\theta} \frac{1}{n} \sum_{i=1}^{n} (1 - \exp(\frac{(e|\theta)^2}{2\sigma^2})). \tag{4.13}$$

Obviously, (4.13) belongs to M-estimation in Sect. 2.1 where Welsch M-estimator $\phi(e) = (c^2/2)(1 - exp(e/c)^2)$ is used. Hence the minimization of CIM can also be viewed as an M-estimation procedure, i.e.,

$$\min_{\theta} CIM^2(e|\theta,0) = \min_{\theta} \sum_{i=1}^{n} \phi(e|\theta). \tag{4.14}$$

4.3 Linear Representation

4.3.1 Linear Least Squares

Linear representation based methods often involve solving a linear least squares problem. In statistics, linear least squares technique is an approach fitting a linear model between data $X \in R^{d \times n}$ and an observation $y \in R^{d \times 1}$. The idealized value provided by the model for any data point in X is expressed linearly in terms of the unknown parameters $\beta \in R^{n \times 1}$ of the model. Generally, linear least squares technique is the problem of approximately solving an overdetermined system of linear equations,

$$\sum_{j=1}^{n} X_{ji}\beta_i = y_j, \tag{4.15}$$

of d linear equations in n unknown coefficients. Equation (4.15) can be written in the following matrix form:

$$X\beta = y. \tag{4.16}$$

Such a system usually has no solution, so the goal is instead to find the coefficients β which fit the equation well in the sense of solving one of the following two minimization problems:

$$\min_{\beta} \|X\beta - y\|_2^2 + \lambda \|\beta\|_2^2, \tag{4.17}$$

and

$$\min_{\beta} \|\beta\|_2^2 \quad s.t. \, X\beta = y. \tag{4.18}$$

If we take a derivative with respect to β in (4.17) and set the solution to zero, we obtain the analytic solution (4.17) as follows:

$$\beta = (X^T X + \lambda I)^{-1} X^T y. \tag{4.19}$$

And by using Lagrangian multiplier method, we can rewrite (4.18) as

$$J(\beta) = \beta^T \beta - \Lambda^T (X\beta - y), \tag{4.20}$$

where $\Lambda \in R^{d \times 1}$ is the Lagrangian multiplier. Take the derivative of this with respect to β and use the quality constraint $X\beta = y$; we have

$$\partial J(\beta)/\partial \beta = \beta - X^T \Lambda = 0 \Rightarrow X\beta - XX^T \Lambda = 0$$
$$\Rightarrow y - XX^T \Lambda = 0 \Rightarrow \Lambda = (XX^T)^{-1} y.$$

Then the analytic solution (4.18) takes the form

$$\beta = X^T(XX^T)^{-1}y. \tag{4.21}$$

When there is a set of feasible solution $\hat{\beta}$ satisfying $X\hat{\beta} = y$, both (4.17) and (4.18) find a solution to minimize $\|\beta\|_2^2$.

4.3.2 Linear Representation Classification

To seek the best representation for the test sample y in class c, the nearest neighbor classifier finds the nearest training sample in that class. That is, it computes the minimal distance between y and all training samples of class c:

$$r_c^{NN}(y) = \min_{x_i^c} \|y - x_i^c\|_2, \tag{4.22}$$

where $\|.\|_2$ denotes the ℓ_2-norm.

Compared with the nearest neighbor algorithm, linear representation methods seek the best representation by samples in each class. Among them, the simplest one is the nearest feature line (NFL) [94] that aims to extend the capacity of prototype features by computing a linear function to interpolate and extrapolate each sample pair belonging to the same class. In NFL, the distance is defined as follows:

$$r_c^{NFL}(y) = \min_{x_1^c, x_2^c, \beta_1} \|y - \beta_1 x_1^c - (1 - \beta_1)x_2^c\|_2, \tag{4.23}$$

where $\beta_1 \in \mathbb{R}$. We can also rewrite (4.23) as follows:

$$r_c^{NFL}(y) = \min_{x_1^c, x_2^c, \beta_1, \beta_2} \|y - (\beta_1 x_1^c + \beta_2 x_2^c)\|_2 \quad s.t. \ \beta_1 + \beta_2 = 1. \tag{4.24}$$

Modified based on [94], Fig. 4.2 gives a geometric illustration of the nearest feature line.

Fig. 4.2 An illustration of the nearest feature line

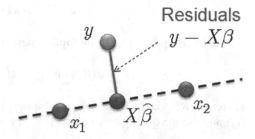

If we extend (4.24) to a higher dimensional space, we get the following optimization problem:

$$r_c^{NCLC}(y) = \min_{\beta^c} ||y - X_c\beta^c||_2 \quad s.t. \sum_{i=1}^{n_c} \beta_i^c = 1. \tag{4.25}$$

Local subspace classifier [88] solves (4.25) by assuming X_c is orthonormal. The nearest constrained linear combination (NCLC) algorithm [93] and K-local hyperplane (HKNN) algorithm [147] solve (4.25) from a different geometric point of view. Note that by removing the equality constraint, we get

$$r_c^{NLC}(y) = \min_{\beta^c} ||y - X_c\beta^c||_2. \tag{4.26}$$

The analytical solution of (4.26) can be directly computed by

$$\beta^c = (X_c^T X_c)^{-1} X_c^T y. \tag{4.27}$$

Figure 4.3 gives a geometric explanation of (4.26) and (4.27).

Fig. 4.3 An illustration of the nearest linear combination

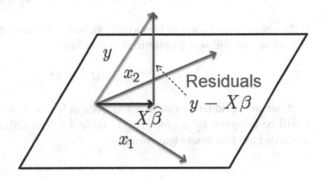

The nearest linear combination (NLC) [93] solves (4.26) by a pseudo-inverse matrix and LRC [109] solves (4.26) by (4.27). LRC simply makes use of the downsampled images for the linear regression classification to achieve the state-of-the-art results as compared to the benchmark techniques [109]. Partial within-class match (PWCM) method [85, 86] solves (4.26) based on partial unterminated pixels. The PWCM further utilizes a robust classification metric based on an M-estimator when all β^c have been computed, i.e.,

$$\arg\min_c ||y - X_c\beta^c||_r \tag{4.28}$$

where $||.||_r$ is a robust norm based on M-estimators.

The minimal residual of (4.26) can also be taken as the distance from a query point to the space spanned by X_c. Then we get the nearest feature space (NFS)

Table 4.1 Different applications of linear least squares

Method	Definition
Nearest feature line [94][58]	$\min_\beta \|X\beta - y\|_2^2 \quad s.t. \; \beta_1 + \beta_2 = 1$
Nearest feature plane [28]	$\min_\beta \|X\beta - y\|_2^2 \quad X \in R^{d \times 3}$
Nearest feature space [28]	$\min_\beta \|X\beta - y\|_2^2 \quad X \in R^{d \times k}, \, k \geq 4$
Linear combination [93][109]	$\min_\beta \|X_c\beta - y\|_2^2 \quad X_c \in R^{d \times n_c}$
Constrained linear combination [93]	$\min_\beta \|X_c\beta - y\|_2^2 \quad s.t. \; \sum_i \beta_i = 1$
Collaborative representation [167]	$\min_\beta \|X\beta - y\|_2^2 + \|x\|_2^2 \quad X \in R^{d \times n}$

algorithm [28] that computes the distance between a query point and its projected point onto the feature space:

$$r_c^{NFS}(y) = \|y_p - y\|_2, \tag{4.29}$$

where y_p is the projection point of y onto the feature space spanned by X_c. According to (4.27), (4.26) can also be rewritten as

$$r_c^{NFS}(y) = \|y - X_c(X_c^T X_c)^{-1} X_c^T y\|_2. \tag{4.30}$$

If the columns of X_c are orthonormal, we have the nearest subspace algorithm [72] that solves the following optimization problem:

$$r_c^{NS}(y) = \|(I - X_c X_c^T)y\|_2. \tag{4.31}$$

After the residual or distance has been calculated, the label of the test sample y will be assigned by $\arg\min_c r_c(y)$. Table 4.1 lists different linear representation methods based on linear least squares.

4.4 Robust Linear Representation via Correntropy

Since large errors will dominate the mean square errors in linear least squares, linear least squares can behave badly when the error distribution is not normal. One remedy is to remove influential observations from the least squares. Then robust linear regression is introduced to employ a fitting criterion to deal with large errors. One of these robust linear regression methods is the correntropy induced loss [48].

By replacing each square error in (4.17) with a robust M-estimator, one has

$$\min_\beta \sum_{j=1}^d \phi((X\beta - y)_j) + \lambda \|\beta\|_2^2, \tag{4.32}$$

where $\phi(.)$ can be any M-estimator in Sect. 2.1. When $\phi(.)$ is Welsch M-estimator, (4.32) becomes ℓ_2 regularized correntropy problem [67]. The problem in (4.32) can be efficiently solved by expending $\phi(.)$ in the multiplicative half-quadratic form

$$\min_{\beta} \sum_{j=1}^{d} (p_j^{t+1}(X\beta - y)_j + \varphi(p_j^{t+1})) + \lambda \|\beta\|_2^2, \tag{4.33}$$

where the weight p_j^{t+1} can be determined by the minimization function of $\phi(.)$:

$$p_j^{t+1} = \delta((X\beta^t - y)_j). \tag{4.34}$$

When p_j^{t+1} is given, the analytic solution of (4.33) takes the following form:

$$\beta^{t+1} = (X^T P^{t+1} X + \lambda I)^{-1} X^T P^{t+1} y, \tag{4.35}$$

where P^{t+1} is a diagonal matrix whose diagonal element $P_{jj}^{t+1} = p_j^{t+1}$. Algorithm 3 summarizes the alternative minimization procedure of (4.32). When there are larger errors in observation y, the minimization function $\delta(.)$ will give small weights to these errors so that the errors have small contributions in (4.33). As a result, the optimal solution of (4.33) is robust to large errors.

Algorithm 3 Half-Quadratic Algorithm for ℓ_2 Regularized Correntropy

---

1: **Input:**data matrix X, matrix G, and test sample y.
2: **Output:**β, p
3: $\beta^1 = X \backslash y$ and $t = 1$.
4: **while** "not converged" **do**
5:     $p_j^{t+1} = \delta((X\beta^t - y)_j)$.
6:     $\beta^{t+1} = (X^T P^{t+1} X + \lambda I)^{-1} X^T P^{t+1} y$
7:     $t = t + 1$.
8: **end while**

4.4.1 ℓ_1 Estimator and Huber M-Estimator

By replacing $\phi(.)$ in (4.32) with different M-estimators, one has different M-estimation problems. When ℓ_1 estimator is used, (4.32) takes the form

$$\min_{\beta} \|X\beta - y\|_1. \tag{4.36}$$

Since ℓ_1 estimator ($|.|$) has a weighting function ($1/|.|$), (4.36) can be solved by Algorithm 3. However, when there is a solution $\hat{\beta}$ that satisfies $X\hat{\beta} = y$, Algorithm 3 will fail to find the real solution $\hat{\beta}$. This is because the weighting function ($1/|.|$) of ℓ_1 estimator will become unpredictable when $X\beta - y = 0$. Since ℓ_1 estimator is not smooth around the origin 0, the minimization of ℓ_1 estimator is still difficult.

Instead of solving (4.36), one often solves the following Huber M-estimation problem:

$$\min_{\beta} \sum_{j=1}^{d} \phi_H^{\lambda}((X\beta - y)_j), \tag{4.37}$$

where $\phi_H^{\lambda}(.)$ is the Huber M-estimator in Table 2.2. Li and Swetits [95] show that the dual solution of the Huber M-estimator problem (4.37) with a small tuning parameter is the least norm solution of the dual problem of the linear ℓ_1 estimation problem (4.36). Moreover, they also show that a linear ℓ_1 estimator can be computed by repeatedly solving Huber M-estimator problems.

Actually, there is a dual relationship between Huber and ℓ_1 estimator, i.e.,

$$\phi_H^{\lambda}(t) = \min_{e}\{(t - e)^2 + \lambda |e|\}, \tag{4.38}$$

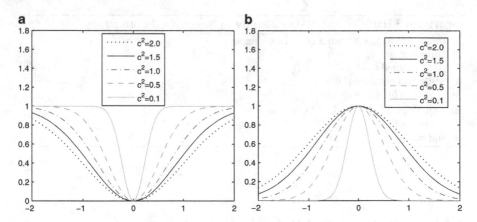

Fig. 4.4 Welsch M-estimator and its weighting function as a function of parameter c^2 in Table 2.2. (**a**) Welsch M-estimator; (**b**) weighting function

which is uniquely determined by the minimization function of Huber loss function in Table 2.2 (or named soft thresholding function in compressed sensing). That is, ℓ_1 estimator is the dual potential function of Huber loss function [112]. Then one has the following equivalence Huber M-estimation problem:

$$\min_{\beta} \sum_{j=1}^{d} \phi_H^{\lambda}((X\beta - y)_j) = \min_{\beta,e} \|X\beta - y + e\|_2^2 + \lambda \|e\|_1. \tag{4.39}$$

When one aims to solve the left part ℓ_1 problem in (4.39) by using soft thresholding function, one actually solves the Huber M-estimation problem rather than the ℓ_1 estimation problem. In addition, the ℓ_1-norm in (4.39) plays a role of Huber M-estimator rather than an approximation of ℓ_0-norm. Parameter λ determines the bandwidth of outliers.

When parameter λ in (4.39) is a fixed constant, Huber M-estimator is a convex function such that (4.39) has a global solution. However, λ becomes a variable when the level of corruptions is unknown. That means that one often faces the following M-estimation problem:

$$\min_{\beta,\lambda} \sum_{j=1}^{d} \phi_H^{\lambda}((X\beta - y)_j), \tag{4.40}$$

or

$$\min_{\beta,e,\lambda} \|X\beta - y + e\|_2^2 + \lambda \|e\|_1. \tag{4.41}$$

When λ is a variable, the above two minimization problems are not convex anymore. In Table 2.2, each M-estimator has a constant parameter to control robustness. Hence parameter selection is an important issue in M-estimation.

4.4.2 Parameter Selection

In M-estimation, the parameter in a robust M-estimator is often set to be a descending sequence rather than a constant. Figure 4.4 shows an example of Welsch M-estimator $(1 - exp(-x^2/c^2))$ and its weighting function $(exp(-x^2/c^2))$ as a function of parameter c^2. We observe that the curve of Welsch M-estimator becomes narrow as parameter c^2 decreases. This indicates that small items in residual $X\beta - y$ are treated as outliers. When a descending sequence is used for parameter c^2, Welsch M-estimator can be adaptive to different types of outliers. At the beginning of reweighting stage, a larger value of parameter c^2 makes that Algorithm 3 only treats large items in residual $X\beta - y$ as outliers. At the last several iterations, since $X\beta$

can reconstruct y better, only a small part of residual $X\beta - y$ has large value. Hence a smaller value of parameter c^2 can be used to determine the ground-truth outliers. The curves of the weighting functions of Welsch M-estimator also illustrate the effectiveness of parameter c^2.

There are several ways to determine the parameters of M-estimators. A commonly used way is from robust statistics. One can make use of the median, mean, or Silverman's rule [60] to determine the parameters in each iteration of Algorithm 3. Generally speaking, the performance sensitivity to the kernel parameter in Welsch M-estimator is much smaller than the selection of the threshold parameter in Huber M-estimator due to the smooth dependence of correntropy on the kernel size [99].

4.4.3 Stability of Linear Representation Methods

In linear representation methods [59,93], one often solves the following linear least square problem

$$\min_{\beta} ||X\beta - y||_2^2. \tag{4.42}$$

The optimal solution of (4.42) can be determined by solving the following linear system,

$$\beta^* = X\backslash y, \tag{4.43}$$

or computed by the pseudo-inverse of X [93,139],

$$\beta^* = X^\dagger y, \tag{4.44}$$

where $\dagger$ is the pseudo-inverse of a matrix. Since X^TX may be singular and is not invertible, ℓ_2 regularization is often imposed on (4.42). And hence the optimal solution is also computed by

$$\beta^* = (X^TX + \lambda I)^{-1}X^Ty, \tag{4.45}$$

where λ is a positive regularization parameter and I is an identity matrix. In matrix perturbation theory [142], one has the following Lemma about the perturbation of (4.42):

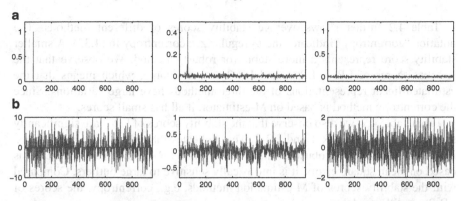

Fig. 4.5 Linear representations computed by different methods (From *left to right*: LR-1, LR-2, and LR-3). LR-1, LR-2, and LR-3 indicate the least square solutions computed by (4.43), (4.44), and (4.45), respectively. λ in (4.45) is set to 1. (**a**) Linear representations computed on an uncorrupted input sample y. (**b**) Linear representations computed on a corrupted input sample y that is generated by corrupting 1 % entries of the input sample used in (**a**)

Lemma 4.1. *If $\beta = X^\dagger y$ and $\beta + h = X^\dagger(y+e)$, then*

$$\frac{\|h\|_2}{\|\beta\|_2} \le k\eta \frac{\|XX^\dagger e\|_2}{\|XX^\dagger y\|_2}, \tag{4.46}$$

where k and η are two constants w.r.t. the matrix X.

According to Lemma 4.1, we learn that perturbation h depends on noise e such that e will significantly affect the estimation of linear coefficient β. We consider that Lemma 4.1 is an agreement with the argument in robust M-estimation that mean square error is sensitive to outliers. Inspired by Lemma 4.1 [142], we introduce the following score to quantitatively evaluate different algorithms' stability and robustness:

$$S_A \doteq \|\hat{\beta}_A - \beta_A^0\|_2 / \|\beta_A^0\|_2, \tag{4.47}$$

where the capital letter 'A' indicates an algorithm and β_A^0 and $\hat{\beta}_A$ indicate the computed coefficients by algorithm A without and with outliers, respectively. The score in (4.47) is also called normalized ℓ_2 error in phase transition diagram [40,42].

Figure 4.5 plots linear representations computed by different methods on uncorrupted data and corrupted data. The corrupted input sample y is generated by corrupting 1 % entries of the uncorrupted one. LR-1, LR-2, and LR-3 indicate the least square solutions computed by (4.43), (4.44), and (4.45), respectively. We observe that LR-1, LR-2, and LR-3 methods are sensitive to outliers. Their linear representations will change significantly even when there is a small level of corruptions.

Table 4.2 further shows average stability scores of different methods. The notation "correntropy" indicates the ℓ_2 regularized correntropy in (4.32). A smaller stability score represents a more stable (or robust) method. We observe that the stability scores of LR-1, LR-2, and LR-3 are very large, which means that the estimated linear representations of the three methods have large variations. Since the correntropy method is based on M-estimator, it all has small scores.

From Table 4.2, we also observe that the stability scores of LR-3 are significantly smaller than those of LR-1 and LR-2. This indicates that when there are outliers, LR-3 can achieve more robust results than LR-1 and LR-2. However, since LR-3 is based on mean square errors, it is intrinsically sensitive to large outliers. Compared with the stability scores of M-estimation methods, e.g., correntropy, the scores of LR-3 are still very large.

Table 4.2 Stability of Linear Representation Methods

Corruption	LR-1	LR-2	LR-3	Correntropy
0.2 %	89.89±67.81	29.62±16.10	3.45±1.82	1.37±0.35
0.5 %	164.66±103.81	53.31±20.82	6.19±2.50	1.54±0.19
1.0 %	216.17 ±135.94	75.30 ±25.08	8.94 ±3.17	1.57±0.17

Stability scores are computed according to (4.47). A smaller stability score represents a more stable (or robust) method

4.5 Summary

Correntropy is proposed in signal processing society as a novel information theoretic measure. It is derived from Renyi's quadratic entropy and has solid theoretical foundation. In this chapter, we described the fundamental theories and properties of correntropy, and introduced how to use half-quadratic minimization to solve correntropy induced problems. We also discussed some applications of linear regression in object classification as a major application of correntropy. We showed how correntropy can be used to improve the robustness of linear regression and develop robust algorithms for classification. Experiments were given to validate the stability of different linear regression methods.

Chapter 5
ℓ_1 Regularized Correntropy

Sparse signal representation arises in application of compressed sensing and has been considered as a significant technique in computer vision and machine learning [27, 65, 154]. Based on the ℓ_0-ℓ_1 equivalence theory [18, 39], the solution of an ℓ_0-minimization problem is equal to that of an ℓ_1 minimization problem under certain conditions. Sparse representation has been widely applied in image analysis [1, 102], compressive imaging [143, 150], multisensor networks [5], and subspace segmentation [46]. Recent theoretical analysis [153] and experimental results [161] show that even if corruptions are high, one can almost recover corrupted data using ℓ_1-based techniques. So far, all sparse representation algorithms can be basically categorized into two major categories: error correction [153, 155, 161] and error detection [65,67,162]. The former aims to reconstruct the original data during robust learning, while the latter detects errors and learns from uncorrupted data.

5.1 Sparse Signal Reconstruction

5.1.1 ℓ_1 Minimization

Recovering a compressed and sparse signal has been a growing interest in signal/image processing and statistical inference. It aims to find the sparsest solution of an underdetermined linear system $X\beta = y$ [39] where $X \in R^{d \times n}$ is a training matrix whose columns represent a redundant basis (i.e., $d < n$), $y \in R^d$ is an input signal/image vector, and $\beta \in R^n$ is an unknown vector to be estimated. And its canonical form can be defined as

$$\min_{\beta} \|\beta\|_0 \quad \text{s.t. } X\beta = y \tag{5.1}$$

© The Author(s) 2014
R. He et al., *Robust Recognition via Information Theoretic Learning*,
SpringerBriefs in Computer Science, DOI 10.1007/978-3-319-07416-0_5

where $\|.\|_0$ denotes ℓ_0-norm that is a count of nonzero entries. Since the problem in (5.1) is NP hard and thus intractable, many approximations of ℓ_0-norm have been proposed. In [23, 34], ℓ_p-norm is used as an approximation of ℓ_0-norm. In [136], correntropy induced metric is further used as an ℓ_0-norm approximator. In compressed sensing, the most commonly used approximator is ℓ_1-norm, which results in the following ℓ_1-minimization problem:

$$\min_{\beta} \|\beta\|_1 \quad s.t. \quad X\beta = y, \tag{5.2}$$

where $\|\beta\|_1 = \sum_{i=1}^{n} |\beta_i|$. Considering that a white noise z satisfies $\|z\|_2 \le \varepsilon$, we can relax the equality constraint $X\beta = y$ in the following form:

$$y = X\beta + z. \tag{5.3}$$

Then the sparse representation β can be computed via basis pursuit denoising (BPDN) method [17, 25]:

$$\min_{\beta} \|\beta\|_1 \quad s.t. \quad \|y - X\beta\|_2 \le \varepsilon. \tag{5.4}$$

By using the Lagrangian method, one can rewrite (5.4) as an unconstrained optimization problem [161]:

$$\min_{\beta} \frac{1}{2} \|y - X\beta\|_2^2 + \lambda \|\beta\|_1, \tag{5.5}$$

where λ is a positive regularization parameter. Iteratively reweighted methods, such as adaptive LASSO [173], reweighted ℓ_1 minimization [19], and multistage convex relaxation [168], are further developed to enhance sparsity for high-dimensional data. And various numerical methods [29, 164] have been developed to minimize (5.4) or (5.5), where the iterative regularization method based on soft-shrinkage operator [116] is often used.

5.1.2 ℓ_1-Minimization via Half-Quadratic Optimization

Many algorithms have been developed for the sparse signal reconstruction in (5.1), such as iteratively reweighted least squares (IRLS) [19, 24, 34], orthogonal matching pursuit [35], gradient projection [50], homotopy [43], iterative shrinkage/thresholding [30, 33], proximal gradient [6], and Bregman iterative [164]. A comprehensive review of optimization algorithms for sparse recovery and compressed sensing can refer to [52, 161, 164] and the references therein.

As in previous sections, we also discuss a general problem for an underdetermined linear system, i.e.,

$$\min_{\beta} \sum_{i=1}^{n} \phi(\beta_i) \quad \text{s.t. } X\beta = y \tag{5.6}$$

where $\phi(.)$ is a loss function in Table 2.2 and can be optimized by HQ optimization. In (5.6), $\phi(.)$ is a smooth approximation of ℓ_0-norm. By using the multiplicative form in Sect. 2.2, we have the following augmented problem of (5.6):

$$\min_{\beta,p} \sum_{i=1}^{n} \left\{ p_i\beta_i^2 + \varphi(p_i) \right\} \quad \text{s.t. } X\beta = y \tag{5.7}$$

where $p = [p_1, \ldots, p_n]^T$ is a multiplicative auxiliary vector, and each p_i is determined by the multiplicative minimization function of $\phi(.)$. And by using the additive form, we have the following augmented problem of (5.6):

$$\min_{\beta,p} \sum_{i=1}^{n} \left\{ (\beta_i - p_i)^2 + \varphi(p_i) \right\} \quad \text{s.t. } X\beta = y \tag{5.8}$$

where $p = [p_1, \ldots, p_n]^T$ is an additive auxiliary vector, and each p_i is determined by the additive minimization function of $\phi(.)$.

In compressed sensing, the optimization problem in (5.7) belongs to IRLS methods [19, 24, 34]. And its analytic solution is [24, 52]

$$\beta^* = Q^{-1}X^T(XQ^{-1}X^T)^{-1}y \tag{5.9}$$

where Q is an $n \times n$ diagonal matrix whose i-th diagonal element is p_i. And by using the Lagrangian method and equality constraint $X\beta = y$, we have the analytic solution of (5.8):

$$\beta^* = Gy + p - GXp. \tag{5.10}$$

where $G = X^T(XX^T)^{-1}$. It is easy to prove that both optimal solutions in (5.9) and (5.10) are feasible solutions to the underdetermined linear system $X\beta = y$.

Then the optimization problem in (5.6) can be solved in an alternate minimization way:

$$p_i^{t+1} = \delta(\beta_i^{t+1})$$
$$\beta^{t+1} = Q^{-1}X^T(XQ^{-1}X^T)^{-1}y$$
$$(\text{or } \beta^{t+1} = Gy + p - GXp)$$

Algorithm 4 summarizes the above optimization procedure.[1] In the half-quadratic step, Algorithm 4 computes a sparse solution p^{t+1} due to the characters of $\phi(.)$ in Table 2.2, and in the least squares step, it finds a feasible solution β^{t+1} according to p^{t+1}. For the matrix G in (5.10), we can only compute it once for a given data X. Hence Algorithm 4 can alternately minimize (5.6) until it converges.

Algorithm 4 Half-Quadratic Algorithm for Compressed Signal Reconstruction

---

1: **Input:**data matrix X, matrix G, and test sample y.
2: **Output:**β, p
3: $\beta^1 = X \backslash y$ and $t = 1$.
4: **while** "not converged" **do**
5:     **Half-quadratic step**: $p_i^{t+1} = \delta(\beta_i^{t+1})$.
6:     **Least squares step**:
    (a) For the multiplicative form, update β^{t+1} according to (5.9);
    (b) For the additive form, update β^{t+1} according to (5.10).
7:     **Parameter step**:
    For the additive form, update parameters according to (5.11).
8:     $t = t + 1$.
9: **end while**

Since the inverse of auxiliary variable p_i is used in the multiplicative form, we only discuss " ℓ_1-ℓ_2', " "Fair," and "Huber" loss functions that have been used in compressed sensing as an approximation of ℓ_0-norm. Considering that the multiplicative minimizers of "ℓ_1-ℓ_2" and "Fair" are the same ones used in IRLS methods [19,52], we fix α in "ℓ_1-ℓ_2" and "Fair" loss functions to 10^{-7}. Inspired by iterative shrinkage/thresholding methods [33], we apply a descending parameter λ in the minimizer function $\delta(.)$ of the additive form-based algorithms, i.e.,

$$\lambda = \gamma \lambda \qquad (5.11)$$

where γ is fixed to 0.99 and the initial value of λ is set to be 0.1. We also use the parameter setting in (5.11) for the multiplicative minimization function of "Huber" loss function.

5.1.3   Numerical Results

In this section, we focus on the reconstruction ability of HQ algorithms rather than the evaluation of which sparse coding method is the best. The abbreviations "**HQA**" and "**HQM**" indicate the additive and the multiplicative forms of HQ, respectively.

---

[1]Code: http://www.openpr.org.cn/index.php/Download/

Since the HQ loss functions are imposed on linear coefficient β rather than errors, Algorithm 4 is not robust to noise.

As in [161], we make use of a given ground-truth sparse signal β_0 to evaluate different methods. If the ℓ_2-norm difference between β^t and β^{t-1} is smaller than a threshold, the iteration will stop. In addition, the number of maximum iteration for all algorithms is set to be 500. A random basis matrix X, input vector y, and a small Gaussian noise are generated based on the platform in [161]. Dimension $d = 500$ and sparsity rate $\rho = 0.1$ are fixed. The number of training samples n is varied from 2,000 to 10,000. All of these simulations are averaged over 20 runs.

Figure 5.2 shows sparse representations recovered by HQA-Huber, HQA-ℓ_1-ℓ_2, and HQM-ℓ_1-ℓ_2 under two scenarios (without or with Gaussian noise). When there is no small Gaussian noise (left column), reconstruction errors of HQA-Huber, HQA-ℓ_1-ℓ_2, and HQM-ℓ_1-ℓ_2 are 0.001, 0.0007, and 0.0001, respectively, and sparsity of the three methods are 106, 100, and 100 (the ground-truth sparsity is 100). Under small Gaussian noise (right column), reconstruction errors of the three

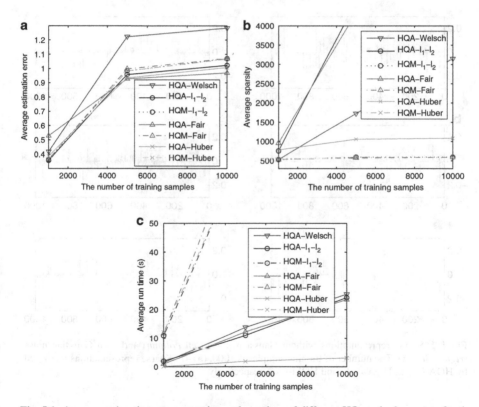

Fig. 5.1 Average estimation error, sparsity, and run time of different HQ methods, w.r.t. a fixed dimension $d = 500$ and sparsity ratio $\rho = 0.1$, and varying n. The abbreviations "HQA" and "HQM" indicate the additive and multiplicative form of HQ, respectively. (**a**) Average estimation error, (**b**) average sparsity, (**c**) average run time

methods are 0.32, 0.32, and 0.32 respectively, and sparsity of the three methods are 609, 777, and 534. Although there are many small nonzero entries in the case of small Gaussian noise, all the three methods almost estimate the nonzero entries of the ground-truth x_0. From Fig. 5.2, we can observe that both of the two HQ forms can be used to reconstruct a sparse signal.

Figure 5.1 further shows average estimation errors, sparsity, and run time of different HQ methods, w.r.t. a fixed dimension $d = 500$ and sparsity ratio $\rho = 0.1$, and varying n. We observe that different objectives result in different experimental results although they are all solved by HQ optimization. Although both two HQ forms based algorithms have similar average estimation errors, they have different sparsities and run times. As shown in Fig. 5.2, there are many small nonzero entries under small Gaussian noise such that the sparsity of some methods is large. And since the multiplicative form based methods involve weighting data matrix X, their computational costs are higher than those of the additive form based methods.

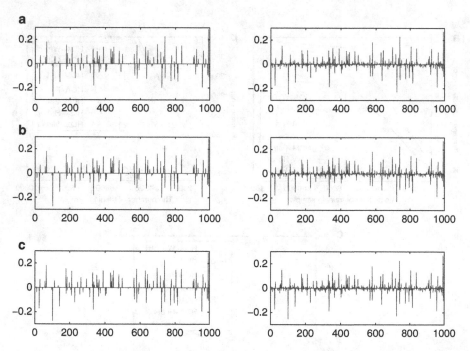

Fig. 5.2 Sparse representations without Gaussian noise (*left column*) and with Gaussian noise (*right columns*). The number of training samples is 1000. (**a**)–(**c**) Sparse representations recovered by HQA-Huber, HQA-ℓ_1-ℓ_2 and HQM-ℓ_1-ℓ_2 respectively

5.2 Robust Sparse Representation

5.2.1 Error Correction

In robust statistics [42] and computer vision [154], the errors incurred by corruptions or occlusions may be arbitrarily large. Hence, one often addresses the following robust model [42]:

$$y = X\beta + e + z, \tag{5.12}$$

where e is a variable describing outliers that are intrinsically different from uncorrupted data, and z is a Gaussian white noise. A number of algorithms have been developed to deal with outliers in (5.12) [65, 154, 161]. They are actually either for error correction or for error detection. The algorithms for error correction are mainly for recovering the ground truth from corrupted data. One representative algorithm in the context of robust face recognition was proposed by Wright et al. [155], which assumes that the error e has a sparse representation and seeks the sparsest solution via solving the following problem:

$$\min_{\beta,e} ||X\beta + e - y||_2^2 + \lambda(||\beta||_1 + ||e||_1), \tag{5.13}$$

where $e \in \mathbb{R}^{d \times 1}$ is an unknown error vector whose nonzero entries correspond to outliers. In [153, 155], (5.13) is often solved by

$$\min_{\omega} ||B\omega - y||_2^2 + \lambda||\omega||_1, \tag{5.14}$$

where $\omega = [\beta^T, e^T]^T \in \mathbb{R}^{(d+n) \times 1}$ and $B = [X, I] \in \mathbb{R}^{d \times (n+d)}$ (I is the identity matrix). The algorithms to solve (5.14) estimate error as a vector variable and correct it in each iteration. And the ℓ_1-norm is an approximation of ℓ_0-norm in order to obtain a sparse solution. Recent analysis and experimental investigations in [153, 161] show that the same ℓ_1-minimization algorithm can be used to recover corrupted data even if the level of corruption is almost arbitrarily large.

5.2.2 Error Detection

The algorithms for error detection are mainly for selecting the most significant pixels (or uncorrupted pixels) in an image for better recognition performance [37, 49, 86]. These methods are often based on robust M-estimators or assume that the occlusion masks are provided, which are widely used in subspace learning and eigen tracking. Recently, based on maximum correntropy criterion [99] and half-quadratic optimization [80, 112], He et al. [65] extended (5.5) by substituting mean square error with correntropy and iteratively computed a nonnegative sparse solution for robust face recognition. He et al. [67] further studied an ℓ_1 regularized correntropy problem for robust pattern recognition, where a robust sparse representation is computed by iteratively solving a weighted ℓ_1-minimization problem. Furthermore, Yang et al. [162] modeled robust sparse representation as the robust regression problem with a sparse constraint and proposed an iteratively reweighted least squares algorithm. Li et al. [96] developed a structured sparse error coding method for continuous occlusion based on the error detection strategy.

To the best of our knowledge, currently there is not a general framework to unify these two kinds of sparse representation approaches aforementioned and study their relationship. For example, although the sparse representation method in [154] indeed improves robustness under tough conditions (e.g., 80 % corruption), the reason why it can work under such a dense error still needs to be further investigated. In the following sections, we will show an HQ framework to unify these error correction and error detection methods.

5.3 Robust Sparse Representation via Correntropy

Based on the HQ framework in Sect. 2.2, this section addresses the following robust problem:

$$J(\beta) \doteq \min_{\beta} \phi_v(X\beta - y) + \lambda ||\beta||_1, \tag{5.15}$$

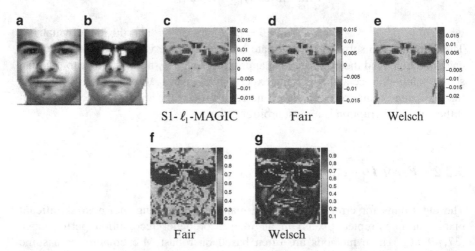

Fig. 5.3 Error and weight images learned by different methods. An error (or weight) image is obtained by reshaping an error vector e or auxiliary variable p. (**a**) An uncorrupted face image in the AR database. (**b**) An input face image y with sunglasses occlusion. (**c**) The error image of S1-ℓ_1-MAGIC. (**d**) The error image of Fair M-estimator-based error correction. (**e**) The error image of Welsch M-estimator-based error correction. (**f**) The weight image of Fair M-estimator-based error detection. (**g**) The weight image of Welsch M-estimator-based error detection

where

$$\phi_v(X\beta - y) \doteq \sum_{i=1}^{d} \phi((X\beta - y)_j), \tag{5.16}$$

and $\phi(.)$ is a non-convex (or convex) M-estimator and can be optimized by HQ. (5.15) can be viewed as a robust formulation of (5.5) by substituting ℓ_2-norm with $\phi_v(.)$. When $\phi(.)$ is Welsch M-estimator, (5.15) is actually based on maximum correntropy criterion. Since $\phi(.)$ is a robust M-estimator, the minimization of (5.15) is actually a robust estimation of β. We adopt the two forms of HQ to optimize (5.15). When the additive form is used, we gain an ℓ_1 regularized error correction algorithm. The auxiliary variable of HQ actually models errors incurred by noise. When the multiplicative form is used, we obtain an ℓ_1 regularized error detection algorithm. The auxiliary variable can be viewed as a weight to detect noise. The following will detail the technique respectively.

5.3.1 Error Correction

In this subsection, we utilize the additive form of HQ to optimize (5.15). Let $Q_v(X\beta - y, p) = \|X\beta - y - p\|_2^2$, we have the following augmented objective function of (5.15) [80, 112]:

$$J_A(\beta, p) \doteq \min_{\beta, p} \|X\beta - y - p\|_2^2 + \sum_{j=1}^{d} \varphi(p_j) + \lambda \|\beta\|_1, \tag{5.17}$$

where auxiliary variable p is uniquely determined by the minimization function w.r.t. $\phi(.)$. When $\phi(.)$ in (5.15) is Huber M-estimator in Table 2.2, the dual potential function $\varphi(p_j)$ in (5.17) is $\lambda_2 |p_j|$. Then (5.15) becomes

$$\min_{\beta} \phi_v^H(X\beta - y) + \lambda \|\beta\|_1 = \min_{\beta, p} \|X\beta - y - p\|_2^2 + \lambda_2 \|p\|_1 + \lambda \|\beta\|_1, \tag{5.18}$$

where the ℓ_1-norm on β is an approximation of ℓ_0-norm, whereas the ℓ_1-norm on auxiliary variable p is the dual potential function of Huber M-estimator. Parameters λ and λ_2 control sparsity and robustness, respectively.

Let $f^{t+1} \doteq p^{t+1} + y$, we can alternatively minimize (5.17) as follows:

$$f^{t+1} = y + \delta_v(X\beta^t - y), \tag{5.19}$$

$$\beta^{t+1} = \arg\min_{\beta} \|X\beta - f^{t+1}\|_2^2 + \lambda \|\beta\|_1. \tag{5.20}$$

Note that, to save computational costs, it will be efficient to only find a solution in (5.20) that satisfies $J_A(\beta^{t+1}, p^{t+1}) \leq \hat{J}_A(\beta^t, p^{t+1})$.

Algorithm 5 summarizes the optimization procedure. As Remark 2 in [112], Algorithm 5 alternately minimizes the augmented objective function $J_A(\beta, p)$ until it converges (Proposition 5.1). In each iteration, it tries to re-estimate the value of an input sample y (f^{t+1}). Since $\phi(.)$ is a robust M-estimator, corrupted entries in y will be corrected step by step. Hence, we denote Algorithm 5 as *error correction*. The minimization subproblem in (5.20) can be solved and expressed in a closed form as a shrinkage [164]. To easily tune the parameters, we give an active algorithm in Sect. 5.3.3 to implement Algorithm 5.

Algorithm 5 ℓ_1 Regularized Error Correction

1: **Input:** data matrix X, test sample y, and $\beta = X^T y$.
2: **Output:** β
3: **while** "not converged" **do**
4:     $f^{t+1} = y + \delta_v(X\beta^t - y)$
5:     $\beta^{t+1} = \arg\min_{\beta} \|X\beta - f^{t+1}\|_2^2 + \lambda\|\beta\|_1$
6:     $t = t + 1$
7: **end while**

Proposition 5.1. *The sequence $\{J_A(\beta^t, p^t), t = 1, 2, \ldots\}$ generated by Algorithm 5 converges.*

Proof. According to the properties of the minimizer function $\delta(.)$ ($\{Q(v_j, \delta(v_j)) + \varphi(\delta(v_j))\} \leq \{Q(v_j, p_j) + \varphi(p_j)\}$), for a fixed β^t, we have $J_A(\beta^t, p^{t+1}) \leq J_A(\beta^t, p^t)$. And according to (5.20), for a fixed p^{t+1}, we have that $J_A(\beta^{t+1}, p^{t+1}) \leq \hat{J}_A(\beta^t, p^{t+1})$ such that

$$J_A(\beta^{t+1}, p^{t+1}) \leq \hat{J}_A(\beta^t, p^{t+1}) \leq \hat{J}_A(\beta^t, p^t).$$

Since J_A is bounded below, the sequence

$$\{\ldots, J_A(\beta^t, p^t), J_A(\beta^t, p^{t+1}), J_A(\beta^{t+1}, p^{t+1}), \ldots\}$$

converges as $t \to \infty$. In particular, $J_A(\beta^{t+1}) \leq J_A(\beta^t)$, for all t, and the sequence $J_A(\beta^t)$ is convergent. $\square$

Similar to S1-ℓ_1-MAGIC, Algorithm 5 also estimates noise at each iteration.[2] However, different from S1-ℓ_1-MAGIC which assumes that noise has a sparse representation as well, Algorithm 5 has no such a specific assumption. If noise

---

[2]We denote the ℓ_1-MAGIC toolbox used to solve (5.34) as S1-ℓ_1-MAGIC.

is indeed sparse in some applications, Algorithm 5 will naturally obtain a sparse solution of p due to the fact that outliers are significantly different from uncorrupted entries.

Figure 5.3d and e show two examples of the auxiliary variables when Algorithm 5 converges. From Fig. 5.3b, we see that there are two occluded regions. One is highlight occlusion and the other is sunglasses occlusion. We see that Algorithm 5 can accurately estimate these two occlusions in this case. This is because M-estimators can efficiently deal with outliers (occlusions) that are significantly different from uncorrupted face pixels. As shown in Table 2.2 in Sect. 2.2, the minimization functions of M-estimators in the additive form can estimate outliers and meanwhile keep the variations of uncorrupted data. In Fig. 5.3d and e, the red regions with large positive values correspond to the highlight occlusion, and the blue regions with small negative values correspond to the sunglasses occlusion.

5.3.2 Error Detection

In this subsection, we make use of the multiplicative form to optimize (5.15). Let $Q_v(X\beta - y, p) = \sum_j (p_j(y_j - \sum_i x_{ij}\beta_i)^2)$, we have the following augmented objective function of (5.15) [80, 112]:

$$J_M(\beta, p) \doteq \min_{\beta, p} \sum_{j=1}^{d} (p_j(y_j - \sum_{i=1}^{n} x_{ij}\beta_i)^2 + \varphi(p_j)) + \lambda ||\beta||_1. \qquad (5.21)$$

According to HQ optimization, a local minimizer (β, p) of (5.21) can be alternately calculated by

$$p_j^{t+1} = \delta(y_j - \sum_{i=1}^{n} x_{ij}\beta_i^t), \qquad (5.22)$$

$$\beta^{t+1} = \arg\min_{\beta} (y - X\beta)^T P(y - X\beta) + \lambda ||\beta||_1, \qquad (5.23)$$

where P is a diagonal matrix whose diagonal element $P_{jj} = p_j^{t+1}$. The optimization problem in (5.23) can be rewritten as the following ℓ_1 regularized quadratic problem:

$$\min_{\beta} ||\hat{X}\beta - f^{t+1}||_2^2 + \lambda ||\beta||_1, \qquad (5.24)$$

where $\hat{X} = \sqrt{P}X$ and $f^{t+1} = \sqrt{P}y$. Note that, to save computational cost, it is unnecessary to find the global solution of (5.24). It may be more efficient to find a sparse solution that satisfies $J_M(\beta^{t+1}, p^{t+1}) \le \hat{J}_M(\beta^t, p^{t+1})$.

Algorithm 6 summarizes the optimization procedure. It alternatively minimizes the augmented objective function $J_M(\beta, p)$ until it converges (Proposition 5.2). Since outliers are far away from the portion of uncorrupted data, their contributions to the optimization of the objective function will be smaller, as they always gain small values in matrix P^{t+1}. Therefore, outliers will have weaker influence on the estimation of β such that Algorithm 6 can compute a sparse representation based on uncorrupted entries in y. And hence, we denote Algorithm 6 as *error detection*.

Algorithm 6 ℓ_1 Regularized Error Detection

1: **Input:** data matrix X, test sample y, and $\beta = X^T y$.
2: **Output:** β, p
3: **while** "not converged" **do**
4:      $P_{jj}^{t+1} = \delta(y_j - \sum\limits_{i=1}^{n} x_{ij}\beta_i^t)$
5:      $f^{t+1} = \sqrt{P^{t+1}}y$ and $\hat{X} = \sqrt{P^{t+1}}X$
6:      $\beta^{t+1} = \underset{\beta}{\arg\min}||\hat{X}\beta - f^{t+1}||_2^2 + \lambda||\beta||_1$
7:      $t = t + 1$
8: **end while**

Proposition 5.2. *The sequence $\{\hat{J}_M(\beta^t, p^t), t = 1, 2, \ldots\}$ generated by Algorithm 6 converges.*

Proof. According to the properties of the minimizer function $\delta(.)$ ($\{Q(v_j, \delta(v_j)) + \varphi(\delta(v_j))\} \leq \{Q(v_j, p_j) + \varphi(p_j)\}$), we have the following form for a fixed β^t, $J_M(\beta^t, p^{t+1}) \leq J_M(\beta^t, p^t)$. And for a fixed p^{t+1}, we have $J_M(\beta^{t+1}, p^{t+1}) \leq J_M(\beta^t, p^{t+1})$ such that

$$J_M(\beta^{t+1}, p^{t+1}) \leq \hat{J}_M(\beta^t, p^{t+1}) \leq \hat{J}_M(\beta^t, p^t).$$

Since J_A is bounded below, the sequence

$$\{\ldots, J_M(\beta^t, p^t), J_M(\beta^t, p^{t+1}), J_M(\beta^{t+1}, p^{t+1}), \ldots\}$$

converges as $t \rightarrow \infty$. In particular, $J_M(\beta^{t+1}) \leq J_M(\beta^t)$, for all t, and the sequence $J_M(\beta^t)$ is convergent. $\square$

Figure 5.3f and g show two examples of auxiliary variables when Algorithm 6 converges. We see that Algorithm 6 treats the two occlusions in the same way. It assigns the two occluded regions small values (weights) due to the robustness of M-estimators. The auxiliary variable in Algorithms 6 actually plays a role of weighting function in each iteration.

5.3.3 An Active Set Algorithm

In this section, we detail the implementations of Algorithm 5 and 6 based on [67]. The optimization problems in (5.20) and (5.24) can be reformulated as the following ℓ_1 regularized quadratic problem:

$$\min_{\beta} \tfrac{1}{2}\beta^T \hat{X}^T \hat{X} \beta - (\hat{X}^T f^{t+1})^T \beta + \tfrac{\lambda}{2}\|\beta\|_1 \qquad (5.25)$$

(For (5.20), $\hat{X} = X$). Let θ be a d dimensional vector whose element $\theta_i \in \{-1,0,1\}$ denotes $\text{sign}(\beta_i)$ and F and G be two subsets of $\{1,\dots,n\}$ such that $F \cup G = \{1,\dots,n\}$ and $F \cap G = \phi$. And let F and G be the working and inactive sets in the active set algorithm, respectively. Then we obtain the following partitions of $\hat{X}$, β, and θ:

$$\hat{X} = [\hat{X}_F, \hat{X}_G]\,,\ \beta = [\beta_F, \beta_G]\,,\ \theta = [\theta_F, \theta_G] \qquad (5.26)$$

where $\hat{X}_F \in \mathbb{R}^{d\times|F|}$, $\hat{X}_G \in \mathbb{R}^{d\times|G|}$, $\beta_F \in \mathbb{R}^{1\times|F|}$, $\beta_G \in \mathbb{R}^{1\times|G|}$, $\theta_F \in \mathbb{R}^{1\times|F|}$, $\theta_G \in \mathbb{R}^{1\times|G|}$, and $|F|, |G|$ are the numbers of elements in F and G, respectively. According to the feature-sign search algorithm [89], when θ has been estimated, we can solve the ℓ_1 regularized problem of Eq.(5.25) by solving the following quadratic programming (QP) iteratively:

$$\min \tfrac{1}{2}\beta_F^T \hat{X}_F^T \hat{X}_F \beta_F - (\hat{X}_F^T \hat{f}^{t+1})^T \beta_F + \tfrac{\lambda}{2}\theta_F^T \beta_F. \qquad (5.27)$$

Instead of finding an optimal solution of (5.20) (or (5.24)), we can only find a local solution to decrease the augmented objectives. Algorithm 7 summarizes the optimization procedure.[3] It maintains the working set F of potentially nonzero coefficients in β, their corresponding signs, and the inactive set G of all other zero coefficients. In the feature-sign step, it systematically searches for the optimal working set and coefficient signs to reduce the objective in (5.25). Then it gives a current guess for the active set and the signs and finds an analytical solution $\hat{\beta}_F$ to the resulting unconstrained QP, and then it updates the solution by an efficient discrete line search between the current solution β_F and $\hat{\beta}_F$. In the half-quadratic step, it minimizes the augmented objective according to current β.

5.4 Numerical Results

Many algorithms have been developed to solve robust sparse representation problems. However, different algorithms often obtain different solutions even if they aim to solve the same minimization problem. In this section, we highlight some of the results [69].

---

[3]Code: http://www.openpr.org.cn/index.php/Download/

Algorithm 7 Active Set Algorithm for Half-Quadratic-Based ℓ_1 Regularized Algorithm

---

1: **Input:** data matrix X, test sample y, $p^1 = -1$, $F = \phi$, $\hat{X} = X\sqrt{P}$, $\hat{y} = \sqrt{P}y$, $\theta = 0$, and $\beta = 0$.

2: **Output:** β

3: **Update the working set:** From zero coefficients of β, compute $r = \arg\max_r |\frac{\partial \|\hat{X}\beta - \hat{y}\|^2}{\partial \beta_r}|$.
   If $|\frac{\partial \|\hat{X}\beta - \hat{y}\|^2}{\partial \beta_r}| > \lambda$, then set $\theta_r = -sign(\frac{\partial \|\hat{y} - \hat{X}\beta\|^2}{\partial \beta_r})$ and update $F = F \cup r$.

4: **Feature-sign step:**
   2.1: compute the analytical solution to the resulting unconstrained quadratic problem : $\hat{\beta}_F = (\hat{X}_F^T \hat{X}_F)^{-1}(\hat{X}_F^T \hat{y} - \lambda \theta_F/2)$.
   2.2: Perform a discrete line search on the closed line segment from β_F to $\hat{\beta}_F$: Check the objective value at $\hat{\beta}_F$ and all points where any coefficient changes sign; Update β_F to the point with the lowest objective value.
   2.3: Remove zero coefficients of β_F from F and update $\theta = sign(\beta)$.

5: **Half-quadratic step:**
   (a) For the error correction algorithm, update f^{t+1} according to (5.19), and set $\hat{X} = X$;
   (b) For the error detection algorithm, update p^{t+1} according to (5.22), and set $\hat{X} = \sqrt{P}X$ and $f^{t+1} = \sqrt{P}y$.

6: **Check the optimality conditions:**
   (a) Optimality condition for nonzero coefficients: $\frac{\partial \|\hat{y} - \hat{X}\beta\|^2}{\partial \beta_j} + \lambda sign(\beta_j) = 0, \forall \beta_j \neq 0$
   If condition (a) is not satisfied, update $\hat{y}$ and $\hat{X}$ according to p^{t+1} and go to Step 2; otherwise check condition (b).
   (b) Optimality condition for zero coefficients: $|\frac{\partial \|\hat{X}\beta - \hat{y}\|^2}{\partial \beta_j}| \leq \lambda, \forall \beta_j = 0$
   If condition (b) is not satisfied, update $\hat{y}$ and $\hat{X}$ according to p^{t+1} and go to Step 1; otherwise return β as the solution.

5.4.1 Sparse Representation Algorithms

We categorize the compared methods into two groups. The first group is not robust to outliers, and the second group is robust to outliers.

First Group In our experiments, the first group includes five sparse representation models, detailed as follows:

(1) For the first sparse representation model formed by

$$\min_{\beta} \|\beta\|_1 \quad s.t. \ \|X\beta - y\|_2 \leq \varepsilon, \tag{5.28}$$

we denote the ℓ_1-MAGIC toolbox[4] used to solve (5.28) as S0-ℓ_1-MAGIC.

(2) For the second sparse representation model formed by

$$\min_{\beta} \|X\beta - y\|_2^2 + \lambda \|\beta\|_1, \tag{5.29}$$

---

[4] http://users.ece.gatech.edu/~justin/l1magic/

we denote the feature-sign search (FSS) algorithm [89],[5] fast iterative shrink-age/thresholding algorithm (FISTA) [6], and homotopy (HOMO) [43] algorithm used to solve (5.29) as S0-FSS, S0-FISTA, and S0-HOMO, respectively.

(3) For the third sparse representation model formed by

$$\min_{\beta} ||\beta||_1 \quad s.t. \, X\beta = y, \tag{5.30}$$

we denote the polytope faces pursuit (PFP) [121] method used to solve (5.30) as S0-PFP.

(4) For the fourth sparse representation model formed by

$$\min_{\beta} ||X\beta - y||_2^2 + \lambda \sum_i w_i |\beta_i|, \tag{5.31}$$

where $w = [w_1,\ldots,w_n]$ is a weight vector, we denote the method used to solve the above adaptive LASSO problem [173] as S0-ALASSO.

(5) For the fifth sparse representation model formed by

$$\min_{\beta} \sum_i w_i |\beta_i| \quad s.t. \, X\beta = y, \tag{5.32}$$

we denote the method used to solve the above reweighted ℓ_1-minimization problem [19] as S0-ℓ_1-W.

In addition, we also compare three linear representation methods. In the half-quadratic minimization for image processing, one considers the following model to deal with white Gaussian noise:

$$\min_{\beta} ||X\beta - y||_2^2 + \lambda \sum_i \phi(\beta_i - \beta_{i+1}), \tag{5.33}$$

where $\phi(x) = \sqrt{\varepsilon + x^2}$ is a half-quadratic loss function. And the regularization in (5.33) models the first-order differences between neighboring elements in β. We denote the additive form and the multiplicative form to (5.33) as HQSA and HQSM, respectively. Linear regression based classification (LRC) [109] and collaborative representation-based classification (CRC) [167] are also compared.

Second Group The second group consists of three robust sparse representation models detailed as follows:

(1) For the first sparse representation model formed by

$$\min_{\beta,e} ||\beta||_1 + ||e||_1 \quad s.t. \, ||X\beta + e - y||_2 \le \varepsilon, \tag{5.34}$$

we denote the ℓ_1-MAGIC toolbox used to solve (5.34) as S1-ℓ_1-MAGIC.

---

[5]http://redwood.berkeley.edu/bruno/sparsenet/

(2) For the second sparse representation model formed by

$$\min_{\beta,e} \|X\beta + e - y\|_2^2 + \lambda(\|\beta\|_1 + \|e\|_1), \tag{5.35}$$

we denote the method FSS, FISTA, and HOMO used to solve (5.35) as S1-FSS, S1-FISTA, and S1-HOMO, respectively.

(3) For the third sparse representation model in the form

$$\min_{\beta,e} \|\beta\|_1 + \|e\|_1 \quad s.t.\ X\beta + e = y, \tag{5.36}$$

we denote the polytope faces pursuit (PFP) [121] method used to solve (5.36) as S1-PFP.

PFP, FISTA, HOMO, and sparse reconstruction by separable approximation (SpaRSA) [156] methods were implemented by "fast ℓ_1 minimization" MATLAB package [161].[6] We tuned the parameters of all the compared methods to achieve the best performance on the training set and then used these parameter settings on the testing set. Since these methods take different optimization strategies and a corrupted testing set may be different from a training one, different sparse representation methods may obtain different results.

Classifier. Wright et al. [154, 155] proposed a linear classification method for sparse representation, and He et al. [65, 67] developed a nonlinear one. In this section, to fairly evaluate different robust methods, we classify an input sample y as suggested in [155]. For each class c, let $\psi_c : \mathbb{R}^n \to \mathbb{R}^{n_c}$ be a function which selects the coefficients belonging to class c, i.e., $\psi_c(\beta) \in \mathbb{R}^{n_c}$ is a vector whose entries are the entries in β corresponding to class c. Utilizing only the coefficients associated to class c, a given sample y is reconstructed as $\hat{y}_c = X_c\psi_c(\beta)$ where X_c is a matrix whose samples all belong to class c. Then y can be classified by assigning it to the class corresponding to the minimal difference between y and $\hat{y}_c$, i.e.,

$$\arg\min_{c} \|y - X_c\psi_c(\beta)\|_2. \tag{5.37}$$

Algorithm setting. As suggested by [155], we normalized the columns of X to have unit ℓ_2-norm for all compared algorithms. We make use of a robust way to estimate the parameters of M-estimators. For Huber M-estimator, the threshold parameter is estimated as a function of median, i.e.,

$$\lambda = a \times \underset{j}{median}(|y_j - \sum_{i=1}^{n} x_{ij}\beta_i^t|). \tag{5.38}$$

---

[6]http://www.eecs.berkeley.edu/~yang/software/l1benchmark/

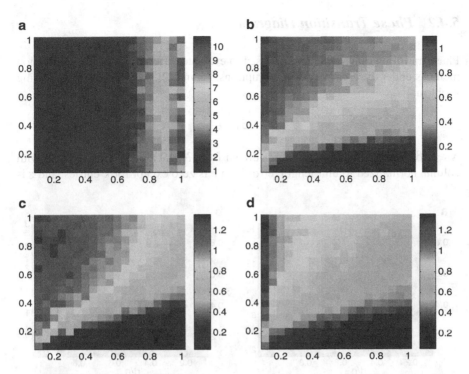

Fig. 5.4 Phase transition diagrams of different methods under different levels of Sparsity, where the level of corruption is fixed at 10 % and the number of samples n is fixed at 200. *Horizontal axis*: $\delta = d/n$ (the number of feature dimension/the number of samples). *Vertical axis*: $\rho = s/d$ (the number of nonzero elements/the number of feature dimension). Each color indicates a different median of normalized l_2 error of $\|\hat{\beta} - \beta_0\|_2 / \|\beta_0\|_2$ over 30 runs. (a) S0-ℓ_1-MAGIC, (b) S1-ℓ_1-MAGIC, [69], (c) Huber-A, (d) Huber-M

And the kernel size of other M-estimators is estimated as a function of mean [65],.i.e.,

$$\sigma^2 = a \times \underset{j}{mean}((y_j - \sum_{i=1}^{n} x_{ij}\beta_i^l)^2). \tag{5.39}$$

The constant a in (5.38) and (5.39) is empirically set to be 0.8 and 0.5, respectively. There are various strategies for the implementation of Algorithms 5 and 6. Here we implement them by the active set algorithm in Sect. 5.3.3.

5.4.2 Phase Transition Diagrams

Phase transition diagram [40, 42] is used to evaluate different sparse representation methods under different levels of corruptions. As in [42], we address the following problem:

$$y = X\beta_0 + e + z$$

where β_0 is zero except for s entries drawn from $N(0,1)$, each $X_{ij} \sim N(0,1)$ with column normalized to unit length, error item e is zero except for k entries, and z is

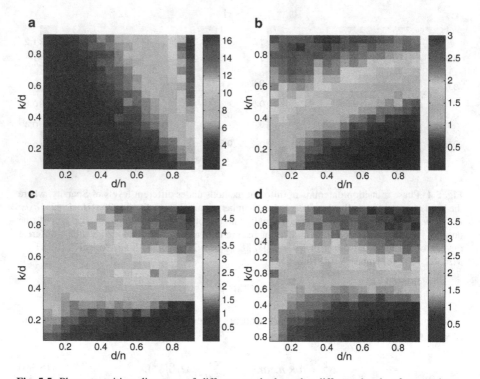

Fig. 5.5 Phase transition diagrams of different methods under different levels of corruptions, where the sparsity s/d is fixed to 0.1 and the number of samples n is fixed at 200. *Horizontal axis:* $\delta = d/n$ (the number of feature dimension / the number of samples). *Vertical axis:* $\rho = k/d$ (the number of corrupted elements / the number of feature dimension). Each color indicates a different median normalized l_2 error of $||\hat{\beta} - \beta_0||_2 / ||\beta_0||_2$ over 30 runs. (**a**) S0-ℓ_1-MAGIC (**b**) S1-ℓ_1-MAGIC (**c**) Huber-A (**d**) Huber-M [69]

small Gaussian noise. To simulate outliers, we draw the nonzero entries of e from $\{2 \times \max_j |(X\beta_0)_j|\} \times N(0,1)$. As in [42], we set white noise z to zero. We perform two simulations. In the first simulation, we vary the sparsity s/d from 0.1 to 0.9 and fix the corruption level k/d to 0.1. And in the second simulation, we vary the corruption level k/d from 0.1 to 0.9 and fix the sparsity s/d to 0.1.

From Figs. 5.4 and 5.5, we observe that S0-ℓ_1-MAGIC fails to deal with large outliers, whereas S1-ℓ_1-MAGIC can control outliers better. Although S0-ℓ_1-MAGIC and S1-ℓ_1-MAGIC are solved by the same optimization method, they are based on different robust models such that they have different robust properties. Phase transition diagrams of the two HQ methods are similar to that of S1-ℓ_1-MAGIC. But the highest normalized ℓ_2 errors of the two HQ methods are larger than that of S1-ℓ_1-MAGIC. Since the two HQ methods make use of a median or mean way to estimate the parameters in robust M-estimators, they can only be robust to a small level of corruption. And when the level of corruption is larger than 50 %, the parameters in robust M-estimators will significantly affect the robustness of the HQ methods.

5.4.3 Sunglasses Disguise

We investigate different methods against sunglasses occlusion. For training, we used 952 nonoccluded frontal view images (about 8 faces for each subject) with varying facial expressions in the AR database. Figure 5.3a shows an example of selected images of the first subject. For testing, we evaluated the methods on the images occluded by sunglasses. Figure 5.3b shows a facial image from the testing set. Figure 5.6 shows the recognition performance of different methods using different downsampled images of dimension 161, 644, and 2576 [109, 155] corresponding to downsampling ratios of 1/8, 1/4, and 1/2, respectively.

Figure 5.6a shows experimental results of the methods that are not robust to outliers. Although these "S0-" methods all aim to find a sparse solution, they obtain different recognition rates, as similarly shown in [161]. This is because they take different strategies for optimization and the corruption level in the testing set is unknown such that one cannot tune parameters of each method to obtain the same result for each testing sample. We also see that sparse representation methods outperform linear presentation methods (HQSA, HQSM, LRC, and CRC). In addition, HQSA and HQSM perform slightly better than LRC and CRC.

Figure 5.6b plots the results of different sparse representation methods that are robust to outliers. Comparing Fig. 5.6b with Fig. 5.6a, we see that recognition rates in Fig. 5.6b are obviously higher than those in Fig. 5.6a. Although the same ℓ_1-minimization methods are used, one "S1-" method can deal with outliers better than its corresponding "S0-" method. The recognition rate of S1-ℓ_1-MAGIC is twice higher than that of S0-ℓ_1-MAGIC. The results in Figs. 5.6a and b suggest that ℓ_1-minimization methods "S0-" fail to deal with the outliers that are significantly different from the uncorrupted data. If outliers are not corrected, they will affect the estimation of sparsity largely. And if outliers are corrected as in the "S1-" methods, the estimated sparse representation can be more accurate.

Figure 5.6c and d show the results computed by the additive form (Algorithm 5) and the multiplicative form (Algorithm 6), respectively. We observe that recognition rates of the additive and multiplicative forms using the same M-estimator are very close. As shown in [65], S1-ℓ_1-MAGIC is not robust enough to contiguous occlusion for face recognition. As the results shown in Fig. 5.6, we observe that algorithms based on Welsch M-estimator significantly outperform S1-ℓ_1-MAGIC and other methods. This is due to the fact that Welsch M-estimator places the same penalties to the outliers incurred by sunglasses. This is consistent with the results reported in correntropy [65, 99] and M-estimation [172] where Welsch M-estimator (or non-convex M-estimators) has shown to be an efficient tool for big outliers and non-Gaussian noise. We can also observe that error correction algorithms (or error detection algorithms) based on Huber and Fair M-estimator achieve similar recognition accuracy as compared with S1-ℓ_1-MAGIC. This is because they all make use of the absolute function in their objectives.

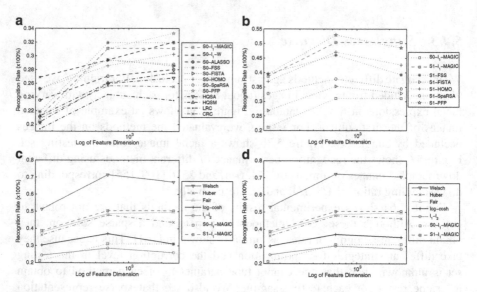

Fig. 5.6 Recognition rates of different methods against sunglasses occlusion in the AR database. (**a**) Recognition rates of the methods that are not robust to outliers. (**b**) Recognition rates of the sparse representation methods that are robust to outliers. (**c**) M-estimators are optimized by the additive form (Algorithm 5). (**d**) M-estimators are optimized by the multiplicative form (Algorithm 6) [69]

5.4.4   Parameter Setting, Sparsity, and Robustness

In real-world applications, the level of occlusion and corruption is often unknown. Hence, a parameter obtained from cross-validation on uncorrupted training set may not be realistic for corrupted testing data. A common way for parameter selection of M-estimators is robust parameter selection method, such as median [37] and Silverman's rule [99]. However, those robust parameter selection methods are only developed for small level of corruptions. When the corruption and occlusion are larger than 50 %, those methods will fail. There seems few existing works to discuss the parameter selection of M-estimators for large corruptions. Facing this difficulty, we follow the approach in [99] to investigate parameter selection and discuss its effect on the performance in terms of robustness and sparsity of coefficient β.

The Extended Yale B Face Database is used to evaluate the performance. For each subject, half of the images were randomly selected for training, and the rest half were for testing. The training and testing set contained 1,205 and 1,209 images, respectively. Each image was resized to 24×21[7] and stacked into a 504-D vector. Each test image was corrupted by replacing a set of randomly selected pixels with a random pixel value which follows a uniform distribution over [0, 255]. The percentage of corrupted image pixels is 10 % and 80 %.

The recognition accuracy and sparsity of Huber and Welsch M-estimator-based robust sparse representation methods are plotted in Figs. 5.7 and 5.8 as a function of the value of a (in (5.38) and (5.39)), respectively. Capital letters "A" and "M" indicate the additive and the multiplicative forms, respectively. The main observations in [69] are summarized below.

Parameter selection: As discussed in correntropy, the kernel size of Welsch M-estimator controls all properties of robustness [99]. We can see that for the two selected M-estimators, their parameters control recognition rates and sparsity of coefficient β. Moreover, the effect of their parameters seems to be different under different levels of corruptions. In the case of 10 % corruption, the best accuracy is achieved when a is around 1.2, suggesting the use of a large a; in the case of 80 % corruption, the best accuracy is achieved when a is around 0.3, suggesting the use of a small a. When the percentage of corruption or occlusion is smaller than 50 %, the mean (or median) is mainly dominated by uncorrupted pixels, and therefore a can be set to a larger value to adapt to uncorrupted pixels; when the level of corruption is larger than 50 %, the mean (or median) is mainly dominated by corrupted pixels, and therefore a can be set to a smaller value to punish outliers.

Sparsity: From Figs. 5.7 and 5.8, we see that outliers will significantly affect the estimation of sparse representation. For all the compared methods, the estimation errors of β increase as the level of corruption increases. Although M-estimators do not directly penalize the sparse coefficient β, they control uncorrupted pixels during learning. In each iteration, robust methods make use of uncorrupted pixels to estimate corrupted pixels. For the additive form, the corrupted pixels of a test sample are iteratively corrected; for the multiplicative form, the corrupted pixels are eliminated by reweighting. Since the sparsity of coefficient β is related to the linear model which mainly depends on uncorrupted pixels, M-estimators will also affect sparsity.

Convex and non-convex M-estimators: From the experimental results, we see that recognition rates of the multiplicative and the additive forms are close for each M-estimator. And different M-estimators will result in different recognition rates. In the case of 80 % corruption, Welsch M-estimator (non-convex) seems to consistently outperform Huber M-estimator (convex) in terms of recognition

---

[7]The matlab "imresize" function was used to resize image.

rates. Although convex loss functions have a global solution, they do not handle outliers well. In real-world applications, there are often several types of outliers, such as sunglasses and highlight occlusions in Fig. 5.3b. As plotted in Table 2.2, a convex M-estimator gives different errors different loss such that it may give much attention on large errors. In contrast, non-convex loss functions often enhance sparsity for high-dimensional problem [168] or improve robustness to outliers in [172]. Moreover, the study in information theoretic learning [99] shows that the performance sensitivity to kernel size is much lower than the selection of thresholds in M-estimators. Hence the selection of M-estimators is important for robust sparse representation and a non-convex M-estimator may be more applicable.

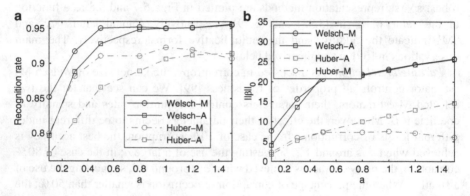

Fig. 5.7 Recognition accuracy and sparsity of Huber and Welsch M-estimator-based methods under 10 % corruption. (**a**) Recognition rate (**b**) Sparsity [69]

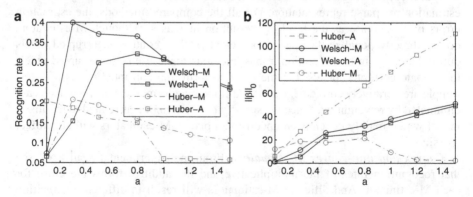

Fig. 5.8 Recognition accuracy and sparsity of Huber and Welsch M-estimator-based methods under 80 % corruption. (**a**) Recognition rate, (**b**) sparsity [69]

Error correction and detection: The performance of error correction and detection is different in the aspects of recognition rates and sparsity, although they optimize the same objective function from the viewpoint of HQ. This difference of the two forms always exists in HQ methods [112]. Note that the augmented objective functions of the multiplicative form is convex only when its auxiliary variables are fixed, which makes local minimum solutions for the pair (β, p). In addition, the recognition rate of error detection algorithms seems to be higher than that of error correction algorithms in a large range of a. Theoretically speaking, the two forms of HQ methods should have similar results if their parameters are well tuned for each testing sample. However, in practice, the multiplicative form is often more robust. This is because the parameter of the multiplicative form seems to be more adaptive and easily tuned for different corruption levels.

5.5 Summary

This chapter mainly focused on robust sparse representation, which is a fundamental problem in compressed sensing. Firstly, the additive form and the multiplicative form of half-quadratic minimization have been proposed to solve sparsity estimation problem in which half-quadratic loss functions are used as an approximation of ℓ_0-norm. Secondly, most of robust sparse representation methods are generally classified into two categories: error correction and error detection. A unified half-quadratic viewpoint has been provided to understand the relationship between the two categories. That is error correction corresponds to the additive form of robust M-estimators meanwhile error detection corresponds to the multiplicative form of robust M-estimators. Based on this viewpoint, new robust sparse representation methods have been developed. Numerical results on different types of errors have shown the improvement from the correntropy based method over the other robust methods in terms of recognition accuracy. It may be also concluded from the results that sparsity and robustness are two coupled problems. How to solve the two problems together and how to evaluate algorithmic robustness and sparsity simultaneously are future directions.

Chapter 6
Correntropy with Nonnegative Constraint

Nonnegativity constraint is more consistent with the biological modeling of visual data and often leads to better performance for data representation and graph learning [66]. In this chapter, we present an overview of some recent advances in correntropy with nonnegative constraint. We begin with an introduction of an ℓ_1 regularized nonnegative sparse coding algorithm to learn a nonnegative sparse representation (NSR). Then we show how to use correntropy to learn a robust NSR. Finally, based on the divide and conquer strategy, a two-stage framework is discussed for large-scale sparse representation problems.

6.1 Nonnegative Sparse Coding

In compressed sensing, one often aims to seek the sparsest nonnegative solution from the whole training set X, i.e., the nonnegative x with fewest nonzeros satisfying $y = X\beta$:

$$\min \|\beta\|_0 \quad s.t. \quad y = X\beta \quad and \quad \beta \geq 0. \tag{6.1}$$

Compared with the sparse coding problem in (5.1) (Sect. 5), each entry of β is further required to be nonnegative. In general, the problem of finding the sparsest solution of (6.1) is also NP hard [14, 41] and very difficult to solve. Fortunately, ℓ_1-norm can be used as an approximation of the ℓ_0-norm if the solution β is sparse enough [14, 41]. Then one can solve the following convex problem to obtain an approximation solution:

$$\min \|\beta\|_1 \quad s.t. \quad y = X\beta \quad and \quad \beta \geq 0. \tag{6.2}$$

© The Author(s) 2014
R. He et al., *Robust Recognition via Information Theoretic Learning*,
SpringerBriefs in Computer Science, DOI 10.1007/978-3-319-07416-0_6

To make (6.2) be robust to small Gaussian noise (white noise), one can further modify the equality constraint in (6.2) by introducing a small constant ε as follows:

$$\min ||\beta||_1 \quad s.t. \quad ||X\beta - y||_2^2 \leq \varepsilon \quad and \quad \beta \geq 0. \tag{6.3}$$

The minimization problem in (6.2) and (6.3) can be solved by orthogonal matching pursuit algorithm [14], second-order cone programming [84], and nonnegative least squares [61, 149]. Based on the Lagrange multiplier method, we can reformulate (6.3) as

$$\min_{\beta} ||y - X\beta||_2^2 + \lambda ||\beta||_1 \quad s.t. \quad \beta \geq 0. \tag{6.4}$$

We denote the method to solve (6.4) as NSR algorithm. Since $\beta \geq 0$, $||\beta||_1 = \sum_i \beta_i$. Then (6.4) can be reformulated as the following quadratic program problem:

$$\min_{\beta} (\tfrac{\lambda}{2} - X^T y)^T \beta + \tfrac{1}{2}\beta^T X^T X \beta \quad s.t. \quad \beta \geq 0. \tag{6.5}$$

The quadratic program in (6.5) is convex because $X^T X$ is a positive semidefinite matrix. According to the Karush-Kuhn-Tucker (KKT) optimal conditions, we can derive the following linear complementary problem (LCP) of (6.5) [123][1]:

$$\alpha = X^T X \beta - X^T y + \tfrac{\lambda}{2}, \quad \alpha \geq 0, \ \beta \geq 0, \ \beta^T \alpha = 0, \tag{6.6}$$

where (α, β) is often said to be a complementary solution of (6.5). If the matrix X has full column rank ($rank(X) = n$), the convex program in (6.5) and the LCP in (6.6) have unique solutions for each vector y.

In order to solve the above problem, we are now introducing an active set based optimization technique. The KKT conditions tell us not all coefficients in α are active. Hence, we divide them into two sets. Let F and G be two subsets of $\{1, \ldots, n\}$ such that $F \cup G = \{1, \ldots, n\}$ and $F \cap G = \phi$. And let F and G be the working set and inactive set in the active set algorithm, respectively. Considering the following column partition of the matrix $X = [X_F, X_G]$ where $X_F \in \mathbb{R}^{m \times |F|}$, $X_G \in \mathbb{R}^{m \times |G|}$, and $|F|$, $|G|$ are the numbers of F and G, respectively, we can rewrite (6.6) as follows:

$$\begin{bmatrix} \alpha_F \\ \alpha_G \end{bmatrix} = \begin{bmatrix} X_F^T X_F & X_F^T X_G \\ X_G^T X_F & X_G^T X_G \end{bmatrix} \begin{bmatrix} \beta_F \\ \beta_G \end{bmatrix} - \begin{bmatrix} X_F^T y \\ X_G^T y \end{bmatrix} + \tfrac{\lambda}{2}$$

where β_F, $\alpha_F \in \mathbb{R}^{|F|}$, β_G, $\alpha_G \in \mathbb{R}^{|G|}$, $\beta = (\beta_F, \beta_G)$, and $\alpha = (\alpha_F, \alpha_G)$. Then the values of β_F and α_G can be computed by the following iterative procedure:

$$\min_{\beta_F \in R^{|F|}} ||X_F \beta_F - y||_2^2 + \lambda \sum_{i \in F} \beta_i \tag{6.7}$$

---

[1] Since β is assumed to be sparse, LCP can be used to efficiently find a sparse active set.

$$\alpha_G = X_G^T(X_F\beta_F - y) + \frac{\lambda}{2}. \tag{6.8}$$

And the optimal solution is given by $\beta = (\beta_F, 0)$ and $\alpha = (0, \alpha_G)$. Algorithm 8 outlines the optimal procedure.

Algorithm 8 ℓ_1 Regularized Nonnegative Sparse Coding Algorithm

---

Input: data matrix X, test sample y, $F = \phi$, $G = \{1, \ldots, n\}$, $\beta = 0$, and $\alpha = -X^Ty$.
Output: sparse code β.
1: Normalize the columns of X and y to have unit l_2-norm.
2: Compute $r = \arg\min\{\alpha_i : i \in G\}$. If $\alpha_r < 0$, set $F = F \cup r$, $G = G - r$.
   Otherwise stop: $\beta^* = \beta$ is the optimal solution.
3: Compute β_F^* by solving (6.7). If $\beta_F^* \geq 0$, set $\beta^t = (\beta_F^*, 0)$ and go to Step 2. Otherwise let r
   satisfy:

$$\theta = \frac{-\beta_r}{\beta_r^* - \beta_r} = \min_i\{\frac{-\beta_i}{\beta_i^* - \beta_i} : i \in F \text{ and } \beta_i^* < 0\}$$

and set $\beta^t = ((1 - \theta)\beta_F + \theta\beta_F^*, 0)$, $F = F - r$,
   $G = G \cup r$. Return to Step 3.
4: Compute α according to (6.8) and return to Step 2.

6.2 Robust Nonnegative Sparse Representation

The nonnegative sparse coding algorithms to solve (6.2), (6.3), or (6.4) are all sensitive to outliers because a larger error will dominate the mean square error. To improve robustness, one can drive a robust model from (6.4) by using correntropy. By substituting the ℓ_2-norm in (6.4), one has the following maximum correntropy problem:

$$J_{CESR} = \max_{\beta} \sum_{j=1}^{d} g(y_j - \sum_{i=1}^{n} x_{ij}\beta_i) - \lambda\|\beta\|_1 \quad s.t. \; \beta_i \geq 0. \tag{6.9}$$

where $g(x) = exp(-x^2/\sigma^2)$. We denote the optimization problem in (6.9) as *correntropy-based sparse representation* (CESR). Since the objective function of CESR in (6.9) is nonlinear, CESR is difficult to be directly optimized. Fortunately, we recognize that the half-quadratic technique [165] and expectation maximization (EM) method [163] can be utilized to solve this correntropy-based optimization problem.

According to Theorem 4.2, we can substitute $g(x) = \max_{p'}\left(p'\frac{\|x\|^2}{\sigma^2} - \varphi(p')\right)$ into (6.9) in a half-quadratic way. Then we have the augmented objective function in an enlarged parameter space:

$$\hat{J}_{CESR} = \max_{\beta,p} \sum_{j=1}^{d} (p_j(y_j - \sum_{i=1}^{n} x_{ij}\beta_i)^2 - \varphi(p_j)) - \lambda \sum_{i=1}^{n} \beta_i \quad s.t.\ \beta_i \geq 0, \qquad (6.10)$$

where $p = [p_1, \ldots, p_d]^T$ are the auxiliary variables introduced by half-quadratic optimization. According to Theorem 4.2, for a fixed β, the following equation always holds:

$$J_{CESR}(\beta) = \max_{p} \hat{J}_{CESR}(\beta, p). \qquad (6.11)$$

It follows that

$$\max_{\beta} J_{CESR}(\beta) = \max_{\beta,p} \hat{J}_{CESR}(\beta, p). \qquad (6.12)$$

Then we can conclude that maximizing $J_{CESR}(\beta)$ is identical to maximizing the augmented function $\hat{J}_{CESR}(\beta, p)$. Obviously, a local maximizer (β, p) can be calculated in an alternating maximization way:

$$p_j^{t+1} = -g(y_j - \sum_{i=1}^{n} x_{ij}\beta_i^t) \qquad (6.13)$$

$$\beta^{t+1} = \arg\max_{\beta} (y - X\beta)^T diag(p)(y - X\beta) - \lambda \sum_i \beta_i \qquad (6.14)$$

$$s.t.\ \beta_i \geq 0$$

where t means the t-th iteration and $diag(.)$ is an operator to convert the vector p to a diagonal matrix. It is clear that the optimization problem in (6.14) is a weighted linear least squares problem with nonnegativity constraint.[2] The auxiliary variables $-p$ can be viewed as weights in (6.14).

Equation (6.14) can be reformulated as the following standard quadratic program:

$$\min_{\beta} (\frac{\lambda}{2} - \hat{X}^T\hat{y})^T \beta + \frac{1}{2}\beta^T \hat{X}^T \hat{X}\beta \quad s.t.\ \beta_i \geq 0, \qquad (6.15)$$

where $\hat{X} = diag(\sqrt{-p^{t+1}})X$ and $\hat{y} = diag(\sqrt{-p^{t+1}})y$. Since $\hat{X}^T \hat{X}$ is a positive semidefinite matrix, this quadratic program in (6.15) is convex. Based on the Karush-Kuhn-Tucker optimal conditions, we have the following monotone linear complementary problem (LCP) [123]:

$$\alpha = \hat{X}^T \hat{X}\beta - \hat{X}^T \hat{y} + \frac{\lambda}{2}, \quad \alpha \geq 0,\ \beta \geq 0,\ \beta^T \alpha = 0. \qquad (6.16)$$

---

[2]According to Theorem 4.2, we can learn that $p \leq 0$. By replacing the p with $-p$, we can get the equivalent minimal problem.

If the matrix $\hat{X}$ has full column rank ($rank(\hat{X}) = n$), the convex program in (6.15) and the LCP in (6.16) have unique solutions for each $\hat{y}$ [123].

Let F and G be two subsets of $\{1,\ldots,n\}$ such that $F \cup G = \{1,\ldots,n\}$ and $F \cap G = \{0\}$. And let F and G be the working set and inactive set in the active set algorithm, respectively. Given the following column partition of the matrix $\hat{X}$:

$$\hat{X} = [\hat{X}_F, \hat{X}_G], \tag{6.17}$$

where $\hat{X}_F \in \mathbb{R}^{d \times |F|}$, $\hat{X}_G \in \mathbb{R}^{d \times |G|}$, $|F|$, and $|G|$ are the number of F and G, respectively, we then can rewrite (6.16) as

$$\begin{bmatrix} \alpha_F \\ \alpha_G \end{bmatrix} = \begin{bmatrix} \hat{X}_F^T \hat{X}_F & \hat{X}_F^T \hat{X}_G \\ \hat{X}_G^T \hat{X}_F & \hat{X}_G^T \hat{X}_G \end{bmatrix} \begin{bmatrix} \beta_F \\ \beta_G \end{bmatrix} - \begin{bmatrix} \hat{X}_F^T \hat{y} \\ \hat{X}_G^T \hat{y} \end{bmatrix} + \frac{\lambda}{2}$$

where β_F, $\alpha_F \in \mathbb{R}^{|F|}$, β_G, $\alpha_G \in \mathbb{R}^{|G|}$, $\beta = (\beta_F, \beta_G)$, and $\alpha = (\alpha_F, \alpha_G)$. Then the values of variables β_F and α_G can be computed by the following iterative procedure [123]:

$$\min_{\beta_F \in R^{|F|}} ||\hat{X}_F \beta_F - \hat{y}||_2^2 + \lambda \sum_{i \in F} \beta_i \tag{6.18}$$

$$\alpha_G = \hat{X}_G^T (\hat{X}_F \beta_F - \hat{y}) + \frac{\lambda}{2}. \tag{6.19}$$

And the optimal solution is given by $\beta = (\beta_F, 0)$ and $\alpha = (0, \alpha_G)$. At each alternating maximum step in (6.14), instead of finding the global solution of (6.14), we simply find a β in the feasible region to increase the whole objective. Combining (6.13), (6.18), and (6.19), we have the active set algorithm for the proposed CESR model.

Algorithm 9 summarizes the optimization procedure[3]. From Step 1 to Step 4, Algorithm 9 finds a feasible β to maximize the objective function for current p^t. In Step 5, Algorithm 9 computes the auxiliary variables of the half-quadratic optimization. The augmented objective function in (6.10) is alternately maximized until the algorithm converges [59]. Note that Algorithm 9 may not reach the maximum value of the correntropy objective in (6.9) because it will return to Step 2 when a feasible solution occurs. Experimental results in [65] show that this solution is good enough for sparse representation based learning problems. Figure 6.1 gives an example of CESR for robust face recognition. It demonstrates that CESR can learn an NSR when there are outliers incurred by sunglasses occlusion.

---

[3]Code: http://www.openpr.org.cn/index.php/Download/.

Algorithm 9 Algorithm of CESR

Input: data matrix X, test sample y, $p^1 = -1$, $F = \phi$, $G = \{1,\ldots,n\}$, $\beta = 0$, and $\alpha = -X^T y$.
Output: β
1: Compute $\hat{X} = diag(\sqrt{-p^t})X$ and $\hat{y} = diag(\sqrt{-p^t})y$.
2: Compute $r = \arg\min\{\alpha_i : i \in G\}$. If $\alpha_r < 0$, set $F = F \cup r$, $G = G - r$.
  Otherwise stop: $\beta^* = \beta$ is the optimal solution.
3: Compute $\bar{\beta}_F$ by solving (6.18). If $\bar{\beta}_F \geq 0$, set $\beta^t = (\bar{\beta}_F, 0)$ and go to step 4.
  Otherwise let r be such that:

$$\theta = \frac{-\beta_r}{\bar{\beta}_r - \beta_r} = \min\{\frac{-\beta_i}{\bar{\beta}_i - \beta_i} : i \in F \text{ and } \bar{\beta}_i < 0\}$$

  and set $\beta^t = ((1-\theta)\beta_F + \theta\bar{\beta}_F, 0)$, $F = F - r$,
  $G = G \cup r$. Return to step 3.
4: Compute α according to (6.19).
5: Update the auxiliary vector p^{t+1} according to (6.13). Return to step 1.

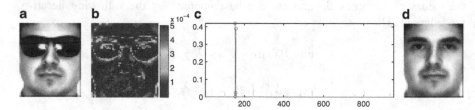

Fig. 6.1 An illustration of CESR for robust face recognition [59]. (**a**) A test face image occluded by sunglasses. (**b**) The weight image learned by CESR. The entry with *blue color* has a small value while the entry with *red color* has a large value. The larger the value of the entry is, the more it contributes to the objective function. Due to the sunglasses occlusion, the pixels around two eyes are assigned small weights, which means that they are estimated as outliers. (**c**) The sparse coefficients computed by CESR. The two largest coefficients correspond to the training images with the same class label of the test image. (**d**) The reconstructed image by the learned sparse linear combination of all the training images

6.3 Two-Stage Recognition for Large-Scale Problems

In some computer vision applications, the number of the samples in data matrix X is often tens of thousands. The computational costs of the robust NSR algorithms in Sect. 6.2 tend to be large as the number of the samples in X increases. In order to tackle the computational cost problem of robust NSR, a two-stage sparse representation (TSR) method is proposed in [61, 68] based on the divide and conquer strategy. Considering the iteratively reweighted procedure in robust NSR in Sect. 6.2, the iterative procedure is decomposed into the outlier detection stage and the sparse representation stage. In the first stage, to deal with varying illumination as well as occlusion, a general multi-subspace framework is proposed in [68] to learn a robust metric via correntropy. Noise and outliers are firstly detected in these subspaces and then a robust metric is learned on the appearance space. In the second stage, to reduce computational costs, an approximation algorithm of the NSR is proposed based on the ℓ_1 ball theory [155]. Then, based on the learned metric, the large-scale dataset is filtered into a small subset according to the nearest neighbor criterion such that a sparse representation can be computed on the filtered subset. This nonnegative sparse solution is unique and can be optimized efficiently.

6.3.1 Outlier Detection via Correntropy

The key point of TSR method [61,68] is to learn a robust metric to detect the outliers and then to harness the NSR to perform classification. Hence correntropy can be used in the first outlier detection stage to learn a robust metric.

6.3.1.1 Learning a Robust Metric

To deal with outliers, one expects to learn a metric M through which outliers are efficiently detected and rejected so that recognition algorithms can work on the uncorrupted subsets of pixels in images. Generally, M is assumed to be a diagonal matrix [157], which can be defined as a function of a test sample y, a subspace $U \in \mathbb{R}^{d \times m}$ that models variation of the dataset X,[4] and a projection coefficient vector $\xi \in \mathbb{R}^{m \times 1}$, i.e., $M \triangleq M(U, y, \xi)$ where $M_{jj} \triangleq \phi(y_j - \sum_{i=1}^{m} U_{ij}\xi_i)$ and $\phi(x)$ is a robust function listed in Table 2.2. Then we obtain the following optimization problem:

$$M^* = \arg\min_{M(y,U,\xi)} \sum_{j=1}^{d} \phi(y_j - \sum_{i=1}^{m} U_{ij}\xi_i). \qquad (6.20)$$

The problem in (6.20) can be optimized in an alternative minimum way [99]:

$$M_{jj}^t = \delta(y_j - \sum_{i=1}^{m} U_{ij}\xi_i^{t-1}), \qquad (6.21)$$

$$\xi^t = \arg\min_{\xi} (y - U\xi)^T (M^t)(y - U\xi), \qquad (6.22)$$

where $\delta(.)$ is the weighting function corresponding to a specific loss function $\phi(.)$ in Table 2.2. The optimization problem in (6.22) is a weighted linear regression problem, and its analytical solution can be directly computed by $\xi^t = (U^T M^t U)^{-1} U^T M^t y$. When $\phi(.)$ is Welsch M-estimator in Table 2.2, the above problem becomes a correntropy problem.

---

[4]Subspace U is composed of the eigenvectors computed by principal component analysis [49].

Algorithm 10 outlines the optimal procedure. According to the half-quadratic optimization [112], Algorithm 10 alternately minimizes the objective by (6.21) and (6.22) until Algorithm 10 converges. Since outliers are significantly far away from uncorrupted pixels, M-estimators will punish the outliers during alternative minimization procedure. When the algorithm converges, we obtain a robust metric in which the diagonal entries corresponding to outliers will have small values.

Algorithm 10 Learning a Robust Metric

1: **Function:** *LRM*(Subspace U, test data y, small positive value ε).
2: **Output:** M and ξ.
3: **repeat**
4:     Initialize *converged* = FALSE.
5:     Update M according to (6.21).
6:     Update ξ according to (6.22).
7:     **if** the variation of entropy is smaller than ε **then**
8:         *converged* = TRUE.
9:     **end if**
10: **until** *converged*==TRUE

6.3.1.2 A Multi-subspace Approach

In real-world face recognition [90, 98], the errors incurred by face disguise are often not random. Face images can be occluded by a monkey image or corrupted by random noise. The errors are often due to the corruption of large region on the human face, e.g., scarf. To deal with this real-world scenario, we develop a multi-subspace approach in this subsection.

Figure 6.2e shows an example of the robust metric learned by Algorithm 10. We observe that although Algorithm 10 accurately detects scarf occlusion, it also treats other important areas around two eyes as outliers. As a result, those areas have smaller values (darker pixels) in the learned metric. Looking at the iterative procedure in (6.21) and (6.22), we find that M_{jj}^t is determined by the reconstructed data $\hat{y} = \sum U_{ij}\xi_i^{t-1}$. If $\hat{y}$ is well reconstructed without the affection of outliers, outliers can be accurately detected. However, since $\hat{y}$ is iteratively computed, it will be potentially affected by outliers especially when there are large corruptions.

To alleviate this problem, Algorithm 10 can be extended in a multi-subspace way. The simple idea is to segment U into $\mathbf{n_u}$ subspaces with the same number of columns ($\cup U^l = U$) where $\mathbf{n_u}$ is the number of subspaces. And then we find a confidence subspace in which outliers only corrupt a small part and can be easily detected. Then an optimal linear coefficient ξ^* is learned on the confidence subset U^l and finally used to reconstruct $\hat{y}$. The final robust metric can be calculated as follows:

$$M_{jj}^* = \phi(y_j - \sum_{i=1}^m U_{ij}\xi_i^*), \tag{6.23}$$

where M_{jj} denotes the j-th diagonal element of subspace M. Assuming that M^l corresponds to U^l and is a subset of M that is computed on U, the confidence subset is determined as follows:

$$l^* = \arg\max_l \sum_j M_{jj}^l, \tag{6.24}$$

where M_{jj}^l denotes the j-th diagonal element of the l-th subspace M. In other words, if a subset is less corrupted, it will receive larger weights than other subsets.

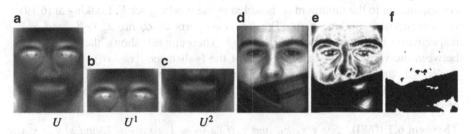

U $\qquad$ U^1 $\qquad$ U^2

Fig. 6.2 An illustration of multi-subspace approach when the number of subspaces is 2 [68]. (**a**) The first dimension of the subspace U learning by PCA. (The vector is reshaped to an image for show.) (**b**, **c**) Two subspaces from U, and $\cup U^l = U$. (**d**) An input face occluded by scarf. (**e**) A robust metric learnt by Algorithm 10 (*Darker pixels* correspond to lower weights). (**f**) A robust metric learnt by Algorithm 11

Algorithm 11 summarizes the procedure of the proposed multi-subspace algorithm. In Step 1, a metric M is learned on the whole subspace and M^l is computed for each U^l. In Step 2, the confidence subspace U^l is determined by (6.24). In Step 3, a confidence coefficient ξ^* is computed on the confidence subspace U^l. In Step 4, we obtain the robust learning metric according to (6.23). An intuitive way to determine the partition of the whole space U is based on the face structure. It is suggested to partition different facial organs into different subspaces. Figure 6.2 plots an example of multi-subspace when the number of partition $\mathbf{n_u} = 2$. Figure 6.2f shows an example of the robust metric learned by Algorithm 11. Compared with Algorithm 10, Algorithm 11 can detect the occlusion on the whole face more accurately.

Algorithm 11 Learning a Robust Metric via Multi-subspaces

Input: Subspace U and $U^l(\cup_l U^l = U)$, a test visual data y, and a small positive value ε.

Output: M.
1: Set $M = LRM(U, y, \varepsilon)$.
2: Find the subspace U^l according to (6.24).
3: Set $\xi^* = LRM(U^l, y, \varepsilon)$.
4: Compute M according to (6.23).

6.3.2   Efficient Nonnegative Sparse Coding

Given a robust metric, we still require an efficient algorithm to find a nonnegative sparse solution on large-scale datasets. In computer vision and pattern recognition [155], each column of the dataset X is often normalized to have unit l_2-norm, which forms an ℓ_1 ball to make the recovery of arbitrary corruption possible [155]. Based on the ℓ_1 ball, we give a deep analysis of Algorithm 8 and try to reduce the computation costs of Algorithm 8.

In Algorithm 8, α_i controls the working set F. In each iteration, the index r corresponding to the minimum α_r is added to the working set F. Looking at (6.19), α_i is composed of three parts. The first two parts of α_i are $x_i^T X_F \beta_F$ and $x_i^T y$, respectively. Here, we denote $X_F \beta_F$ by $\hat{y}$. Theorem 6.1 shows the relationship between the value of $x_i^T y$ and the value of the l_2 distance $||x_i - y||_2$. If $||x_i||_2^2 = 1$, $||x_j||_2^2 = 1$, and $x_i^T y \geq x_j^T y$, x_j will be far away from y than x_i (i.e., $||x_i - y||_2 \leq ||x_j - y||_2$). Based on Theorem 6.1, we categorize the relationship between the value of α_i and the distance from x_i to y into four cases in Table 6.1.

Theorem 6.1 ([68]). *For $\forall$ x_i, x_j, and y, if $||x_i||_2 = 1$, $||x_j||_2 = 1$, and $x_i^T y \geq x_j^T y$, then the inequality $||x_i - y||_2 \leq ||x_j - y||_2$ holds true.*

Proof sketch. *Given that $||x_i||_2^2 = 1$, $||x_j||_2^2 = 1$, and $x_i^T y \geq x_j^T y$, we have $(x_i^T x_i - 2x_i^T y + y^T y) \leq (x_j^T x_j - 2x_j^T y + y^T y)$. Hence, $||x_i - y||_2^2 \leq ||x_j - y||_2^2$.*

For Case 1 and Case 4 in Table 6.1, the λ in Algorithm 8 plays a role of a truncation function. Considering the inequality constraint $\alpha_r < 0$ in Step 4 of Algorithm 8 and the condition $\lambda > 0$, the inequality $x_r^T(X_F \beta_F - y) + \frac{\lambda}{2} < 0$ is equivalent to $x_r^T(X_F \beta_F - y) < -\frac{\lambda}{2}$. This indicates that there may be a sample x_i that corresponds to a large α_i value ($\alpha_i < 0$) and can further reduce the objective. But the nonnegative regularization item λ will restrict this sample from the working set F. In Case 1 and Case 4, we learn if x_i is nearer to y than x_j, α_i will be smaller than α_j. Hence λ plays a role of a truncation function to remove faraway samples ($-\frac{\lambda}{2} \leq \alpha_i < 0$).

For Case 2 and Case 3 in Table 6.1, λ in Algorithm 8 also plays a role of a discriminative function. In (6.19), there are two items that determine the value of α_i. The sample x_i that is near to y may have a large value α_i so that it does not satisfy the inequality in Step 4. However, α_j with respect to a faraway sample x_j can also have a small value. Although a sample may be near to y, it will be potentially restricted from the working set F if it is redundant in the dataset X. Hence λ potentially makes Algorithm 8 compute a discriminate code.

Based on the above four cases, we learn that the ℓ_1 regularizer λ plays an important role in finding a nonnegative sparse solution and also plays the role of a truncation function to remove faraway samples. This indicates that if the nonnegative least squares technique is adopted to compute a sparse solution on the nearest dataset, the solution will be an approximation of nonnegative sparse solution. If a dataset tends to be large, the solution computed by the nonnegative least squares technique in [65,149] without harnessing the ℓ_1 regularization may not

Table 6.1 The relationship between the value of α_i and the distance from x_i to y ($||x_i||_2 = 1$) [68]

	$-x_i^T y$	$x_i^T \hat{y}$ ($\hat{y} \doteq X_F \beta_F$)	$\alpha_i = x_i^T \hat{y} - x_i^T y$
Case 1	$||x_i - y||_2 \leq ||x_j - y||_2$	$||x_i - \hat{y}||_2 \geq ||x_j - \hat{y}||_2$	$\alpha_i \leq \alpha_j$
Case 2	$||x_i - y||_2 \leq ||x_j - y||_2$	$||x_i - \hat{y}||_2 \leq ||x_j - \hat{y}||_2$	$\alpha_i \leq \alpha_j$ or $\alpha_i \geq \alpha_j$
Case 3	$||x_i - y||_2 \geq ||x_j - y||_2$	$||x_i - \hat{y}||_2 \geq ||x_j - \hat{y}||_2$	$\alpha_i \leq \alpha_j$ or $\alpha_i \geq \alpha_j$
Case 4	$||x_i - y||_2 \geq ||x_j - y||_2$	$||x_i - \hat{y}||_2 \leq ||x_j - \hat{y}||_2$	$\alpha_i \geq \alpha_j$

be sparse. Since the datasets used in [65, 149] are not very large and the dimension of dataset is often larger than the size of dataset, the nonnegative least squares techniques in [65, 149] can find a nonnegative sparse solution. Hence the necessary condition for nonnegative least squares technique to find a sparse solution is that the nearest dataset is used. Experimental results in [61, 66, 68] also confirm this finding.

6.3.3 Two-Stage Sparse Representation

Based on the analysis of the role of regularizer λ, we first filter the database into a small subset according to the nearest neighbor criterion in the learnt robust metric. We denote the number of the nearest neighbors by n_{knn} and let $n_{knn} < min(n, d)$ (The n_{knn} is the k in KNN). The motivation of this filtering step lies on three things: (1) it ensures that the following optimization problem in (6.25) has a unique solution; (2) it plays a similar role as λ in LASSO to remove some samples corresponding to small coefficients[5]; (3) it significantly reduces computational costs for large-scale problems.

Secondly, a nonnegative representation is computed on the subset by solving (6.4). For convenience, we set $\lambda = 0$ [149]. Then we have

$$\min ||y - X\beta||_2^2 \quad s.t. \quad \beta \geq 0. \tag{6.25}$$

If the matrix X has full column rank ($rank(X) = n$), the matrix $X^T X$ is positive definite so that the strictly convex program in (6.25) has unique solutions for each vector y [10].

If a truncation function is used to remove faraway samples, some useful information will be lost in Case 2 and Case 3. Fortunately, based on the collaborative character [167] in sparse representation classification(i.e., sparse coding is performed collaboratively over relative datasets), a test sample is assumed to

---

[5]The active set algorithm [11,49] to solve (6.4) selects the sample that can significantly reduce the objective step by step. The lastly selected samples often correspond to smallest coefficients and are far away from the query y.

be represented by a linear combination of the data only from its relative and collaborative classes. Hence we compute an informative and sparse code only from its relative classes.

Algorithm 12 Two-Stage Sparse Representation (TSR)

Input: data matrix X, a test sample y, the number of the nearest neighbor n_{knn}.
Output: β^*.
1: Normalize each sample in X to have unit l_2-norm.
2: Compute a robust diagonal metric M according to Algorithm 10 (or Algorithm 11), and set $\hat{X} = \sqrt{M}X$ and $\hat{y} = \sqrt{M}y$.
3: Compute a nearest subset I^1 in $\hat{X}$ to $\hat{y}$ according to the nearest neighbor criterion, and set $\hat{X}^1 = \{x_i | i \in I^1\}$.
4: Solve the nonnegative least squares problem:

$$\beta^* = \arg\min_\beta \|\hat{X}^1\beta - \hat{y}\| \ s.t. \ \beta \geq 0.$$

5: Set $I^2 = \{i | \beta_i > 0 \ and \ i \in I^1\}$ and $\hat{X}^2 = \{\hat{X}_c | \hat{x}_i \in \hat{X}_c \ and \ i \in I^2\}$, solve the nonnegative problem:

$$\beta^* = \arg\min_\beta \|\hat{X}^2\beta - \hat{y}\| \ s.t. \ \beta \geq 0.$$

Algorithm 12 summarizes the procedure of the TSR. In Step 2, we make use of Algorithm 10 (or Algorithm 11) to learn a robust metric M. And then we set $\hat{X} = \sqrt{M}X$ and $\hat{y} = \sqrt{M}y$ so that we can perform classification under M in the following steps. In Step 3, to reduce computational costs, the large-scale dataset $\hat{X}$ is filtered into a small subset $\hat{X}^1$. In Step 4, a sparse representation is computed by NSR on the $\hat{X}^1$. In Step 5, considering that each object class often has several instances, i.e., $n_c \geq 1$, we select all the instances in the class corresponding to the nonzero coefficients in Step 4 so that we select the most competitive classes. Then the final NSR is computed on $\hat{X}^2$.

If we want to perform classification tasks based on NSR β, we can classify a test sample y as follows [155]. For each class c, let $\delta_c : \mathbb{R}^n \to \mathbb{R}^{n_c}$ be a function which selects the coefficients belonging to class c, i.e., $\delta_c(\beta) \in \mathbb{R}^{n_c}$ is a vector whose entries are the entries in β corresponding to class c. Utilizing only the coefficients associated to class c, the given sample y is reconstructed as $\hat{y}_c = X_c\delta_c(\beta)$. Then y is classified based on these reconstructions by assigning it to the class that minimizes the residual between y and $\hat{y}_c$:

$$\min_c r_c(y) \doteq \|y - \hat{y}_c\|_M, \tag{6.26}$$

where $\|.\|_M$ is the correntropy induced diagonal metric in (6.20).

6.4 Numerical Results

In this section, we highlight some applications of the NSR presented in [61, 65, 66, 68]. Two face databases are selected to evaluate different methods. All facial images are manually aligned and converted to grayscale. The details of the two databases are as follows:

1. *AR Database* [103]: The AR database consists of over 4,000 facial images from 126 subjects (70 men and 56 women). For each subject, 26 facial images are taken in two separate sessions. These images suffer different facial variations including various facial expressions (neutral, smile, anger, and scream), illumination variations (left light on, right light on, and all side lights on), and occlusion by sunglasses or scarf. This database is often used for the evaluation of robust face recognition algorithms. In this section, we selected a subset of this database that consists of 65 male subjects and 54 female subjects. The gray-scale images were cropped to resolution 112×92. Figure 6.3 shows some cropped images in this database.

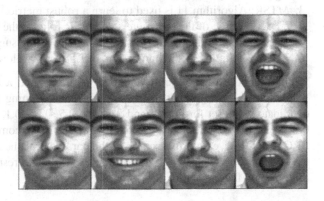

Fig. 6.3 Cropped facial images of the first subject in the AR database. *Top row*: the images from the first session. *Bottom row*: the images from the second session

2. *PEAL Database [53]*: The CAS-PEAL database is a large-scale Chinese face database. For the training set, we selected all frontal facial images undergone expression and lighting variations, where the pose degrees of all frontal facial images are less than or equal to $22°$. Then the training set contains 7,448 images of 1,038 individuals. For the first testing set, we select 261 images of 261 individuals occluded by sunglasses in the accessory dataset. For the second testing set, we select 784 images of 262 individuals occluded by hat in the accessory dataset. The images were cropped with dimension 32×32. Figure 6.4 shows some cropped images in this database.

Six robust algorithms are compared in this section. They are:

1. *SRC*: We compare its two robust models, which are different in the aspects of robustness and computational strategy [155]. *SRC1*: the implementation minimizes the ℓ_1-norm in (5.34) via a primal-dual algorithm for linear programming

Fig. 6.4 Samples of cropped faces in the CAS-PEAL database. *Top row*: cropped facial images in the training set. *Bottom row*: occluded facial images in the testing set

based on [16].[6] *SRC2*: the implementation minimizes the ℓ_1-norm in (5.35) via an active set algorithm based on [89].[7]

2. *TSR*[8]: The n_{knn} in Step 2 is set to 300. The subspace U in Algorithm 10 is composed of the eigenvectors corresponding to the five largest eigenvalues as suggested in [11,49]. Algorithm 10 is used to learn a robust metric.
3. *M*TSR: Algorithm 11 is used to learn a robust metric.
4. *C*ESR: Setting of the parameters of CESR follows the suggestion in [65].[9]
5. *RSC*: Setting of the parameters of RSC follows the suggestion in [162].[10]
6. *LDAonK*: Setting of the parameters of LDAonK follows the suggestion in [49].

In order to estimate the parameter ε of SRC1 and λ of SRC2, fivefold cross-validation on each dimension of data for each training set was used, where the candidate value set for both ε and λ is {1, 0.5, 0.25, 0.1, 0.075, 0.05, 0.025, 0.01, 0.005, 0.001, 0.0005, 0.0001}. Note that due to large computational cost of SRC1, SRC2, and RSC, exhaustive search of the parameter value is not applicable. Also for the same reason, we can only report the experimental results of SRCs in the lower dimensional feature space.

6.4.1 Sunglasses Disguise

The robustness of different methods are studied under sunglasses disguise. The training set is composed of 952 images (about eight for each subject) of un-occluded frontal views with varying facial expressions from the AR database.

---

[6]The source code: http://www.acm.caltech.edu/l1magic/.

[7]The source code: http://redwood.berkeley.edu/bruno/sparsenet/.

[8]The source code: http://www.openpr.org.cn/index.php/All/63-Two-stage-Sparse-Representation/View-details.html.

[9]The source code: http://www.openpr.org.cn/index.php/All/69-CESR/View-details.html.

[10]The source code: http://www4.comp.polyu.edu.hk/~cslzhang.

And the testing set is composed of the images with sunglasses. Figure 6.5 shows the recognition performance of different methods based on different downsampled images of dimension 154, 644, and 2,576 [155]. Those numbers correspond to downsampling ratios of 1/8, 1/4, and 1/2, respectively.

Fig. 6.5 Recognition rates of different methods under sunglasses occlusion [68]

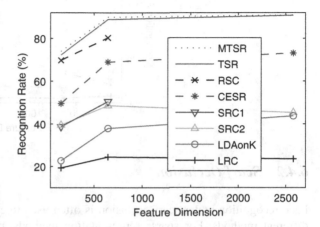

In Fig. 6.5, the methods can be ranked in descending recognition accuracy as MTSR, TSR, RSC, CESR, SRC1, SRC2, LDAonK, and LRC. The sparse representation based methods outperform two non-sparse ones. If occlusions exist, it is unlikely that the test image will be very similar to the subspace of the same class, so that LRC performs poorly. In this case, TSR and RSC, CESR significantly performs better than two SRC methods. As in [162], iteratively reweighted methods seem to deal with outliers better than other methods. MTSR achieves the highest recognition rates. This is because the outlier detection stage of MTSR can efficiently detect the sunglasses occlusion. The MCC in MTSR is robust to non-Gaussian noise [65].

Although TSR, CESR, and RSC are all based on M-estimators (correntropy can be viewed as Welsch M-estimator), they deal with outliers in different ways. Both CESR and RSC find robust weights and solve an ℓ_1-minimization subproblem. Since RSC uses complexity strategy with a large computational cost to detect outliers, it may be more robust than CESR in some cases. Although both TSR and CESR are based on correntropy to detect outliers, TSR can deal with outliers better due to its independent outlier detection step. As a result, TSR outperforms CESR. Since real-world corruptions are often incurred by several types of outliers, the strategy to use M-estimators (including correntropy) will also affect recognition rates.

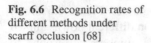

Fig. 6.6 Recognition rates of different methods under scarff occlusion [68]

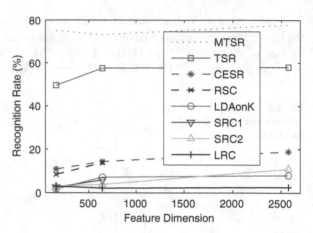

6.4.2 Scarf Occlusion

Face recognition under scarf occlusion is often used to evaluate the robustness of different methods. For sparse representation methods, partition scheme is often used to tackle scarf occlusion [65, 109, 155]. In real-world problems, occlusion and corruption are often known such that we cannot make use of partition scheme in all scenarios. In this subsection, we perform experiments under scarf occlusion. For training, we select 952 images (about eight for each subject) of un-occluded frontal views with varying facial expressions. For testing, we use images with scarf as shown in Fig. 6.2d.

Figure 6.6 shows the recognition rates of eight compared methods. We observe that MTSR significantly outperforms other methods. Although RSC and CESR perform better than two SRC methods, they still fail to detect the errors incurred by scarf occlusion. The reason of low recognition rates is that there is mustache on some facial images. Since the pixels in the mustache area are similar to the pixels corrupted by scarf occlusion, SRCs fail to detect the occluded area and always select the facial images with mustache as the most similar images. Figure 6.7 shows such an example. As a result, the recognition rates of SRCs, RSC, and CESR are quite low. As discussed in Sect. 6.3.1.2, MTSR and TSR make use of PCA subspace

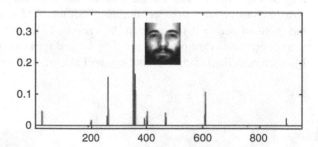

Fig. 6.7 The sparse coefficients learned by SRC1 under scarf occlusion [68]

Algorithm	LRC	MTSR	TSR	TSR1
Glasses occlusion	30.3	**44.0**	40.2	35.3
Hat occlusion	23.1	**54.2**	53.8	45.2

Table 6.2 Recognition rates (%) on the large-scale PEAL dataset [68]

in the outlier detection stage instead of using the whole training samples. This subspace can model facial variations and alleviate the affection of individual sample. Hence MTSR and TSR accurately detect the corrupted region such that they achieve the highest recognition rates. This experiment also suggests that accurate outlier detection is important for robust sparse representation methods.

6.4.3 Large-Scale Problems

In this subsection, the performance of TSR is further evaluated on the large-scale PEAL dataset which consists of 7,448 facial images in the training set. Table 6.2 tabulates experimental results on the two testing sets. Since there are large variations of facial images in the training set and occlusions in the testing set, the recognition tasks are difficult. Hence, recognition rates of all methods are low. Due to the large number of facial images, some sparse representation methods cannot find a feasible solution in available time. Hence we only report the results of LRC method as comparison. In addition, TSR1 denotes the TSR without the filtering steps (Steps 4 and 5), i.e., the TSR1 directly computes an NSR on the whole dataset $\hat{X}$ via nonnegative least squares technique. Algorithm 10 is used to learn a robust metric.

For the first testing set of glasses occlusion, both MTSR and TSR perform better than LRC and TSR1. Although the robust metric in TSR1 is the same as that in TSR, TSR learns an approximation solution of NSR. The coefficients learned by TSR are more informative than those learned by TSR1. As a result, there is a significant improvement in terms of recognition rate. Experiments also confirm that sparse regularization parameter λ plays a role of filter operator that removes the faraway samples from an input observation y.

For the second testing set of hat occlusion, the proposed methods significantly outperform LRC. As expected, MTSR achieves the highest recognition rate. Looking at the sample images occluded by hat in Fig. 6.4, we observe that the hat occlusion incurs large variations of the pixels beyond two eyes. Although the occluded pixels are significantly different from those unconcluded pixels, they only corrupt small parts of one cropped face image. LRC fails to deal with these small occlusions such that it obtains a low recognition rate. However, TSR can accurately detect these occlusions and hence significantly outperforms LRC. Since hat occlusion only corrupts a small area of the whole face image, both MTSR and TSR can accurately detect the errors. As a result, the recognition rates of the two methods are similar.

6.5 Summary

NSR is a fundamental problem in compressed sensing. In this chapter, some recent advances in NSR have been reviewed. Based on the analysis of the role of sparse regularization parameter λ, an efficient nonnegative sparse coding algorithm has been proposed to seek an NSR on large-scale dataset. To improve the robustness to outliers, correntropy with nonnegative constraints has been well studied. A correntropy-based NSR method and a two-stage NSR method have been studied. Experiments confirm that correntropy is a useful and robust estimator to improve the robustness of NSR. Since NSR is still an ongoing issue in compressed sensing, one direction of future work is imposing non-convex sparse approximator to enhance sparsity. Another direction is to apply correntropy-based nonnegative models to other computer vision tasks, such as video surveillance and dictionary learning.

References

1. Aharon, M., Elad, M., Bruckstein, A.M.: The k-svd: An algorithm for designing of overcomplete dictionaries for sparse representations. IEEE Transactions on Signal Processing **54**(11), 4311–4322 (2006)
2. Ahna, J., Oha, J., Choib, S.: Learning principal directions: Integrated-squared-error minimization. Neurocomputing **70**, 1372–1381 (2007)
3. Allain, M., Idier, J., Goussard, Y.: On global and local convergence of half-quadratic algorithms. IEEE Transactions on Image Processing **15**(5), 1030–1042 (2006)
4. Angst, R., Zach, C., Pollefeys, M.: The generalized trace norm and its application to structure from motion problems. In: International Conference on Computer Vision, pp. 2502–2509 (2011)
5. Bajwa, W., Haupt, J., Sayeed, A., Nowak, R.: Compressive wireless sensing. In: Proceedings of International Conference on Information Processing in Sensor Networks (2006)
6. Beck, A., Teboulle, M.: A fast iterative shrinkage-thresholding algorithm for linear inverse problems. SIAM Journal on Imaging Sciences **2**(1), 183–202 (2009)
7. Belhumeur, P.N., Hespanha, J., Kriegman, D.J.: Eigenfaces vs. fisherfaces: Recognition using class specific linear projection. IEEE Transactions on Pattern Analysis and Machine Intelligence **19**(7), 711–720 (1997)
8. Belkin, M., Niyogi, P., Sindhwani, V.: Manifold regularization: A geometric framework for learning from labeled and unlabeled examples. Journal of Machine Learning Research pp. 2399–2434 (2006)
9. Bioucas-Dias, J., Figueiredo, M.: A new twist: Two-step iterative shrinkage/thresholding algorithms for image restoration. IEEE Transactions on Image Processing **16**(12), 2992–3004 (2007)
10. Bjorck, A.: A direct method for sparse least-squares problems with lower and upper bounds, numer. Math **54**, 19–32 (1988)
11. Black, M., Jepson, A.: Eigentracking: Robust matching and tracking of articulated objects using a view-based representation. International Journal of Computer Vision **26**(1), 63–84 (1998)
12. Blake, A., Zisserman, A.: Visual Reconstruction. MIT Press, Cambridge, MA (1987)
13. Boyd, S., Vandenberghe, L.: Convex optimization. Cambridge University Press (2004)
14. Bruckstein, A.M., Elad, M., Zibulevskyy, M.: On the uniqueness of nonnegative sparse solutions to underdetermined systems of equations. IEEE Transactions on Information Theory **54**(11), 4813–4820 (2008)
15. Cai, D., He, X., Han, J.: Spectral regression for efficient regularized subspace learning. In: International Conference on Computer Vision, pp. 1–7 (2007)

© The Author(s) 2014
R. He et al., *Robust Recognition via Information Theoretic Learning*,
SpringerBriefs in Computer Science, DOI 10.1007/978-3-319-07416-0

16. Candés, E.J., Romberg, J.: l1-magic: recovery of sparse signals via convex programming. http://www.acm.caltech.edu/l1magic/ (2005)
17. Candés, E.J., Romberg, J., Tao, T.: Stable signal recovery from incomplete and inaccurate measurements. Communications on Pure and Applied Math **59**(8), 1207–1223 (2006)
18. Candés, E.J., Tao, T.: Near optimal signal recovery from random projections: universal encoding strategies. IEEE Transactions on Information Theory **52**(12), 5406–5425 (2006)
19. Candés, E.J., Wakin, M., Boyd, S.: Enhancing sparsity by reweighted ℓ_1 minimization. Journal of Fourier Analysis and Applications **14**(5), 877–905 (2008)
20. Cetin, M., Karl, W.C.: Feature-enhanced synthetic aperture radar image formation based on nonquadratic regularization. IEEE Transactions on Image Processing **10**(4), 623–631 (2001)
21. Champagnat, F., Idier, J.: A connection between half-quadratic criteria and EM algorithms. IEEE Signal Processing Letters **11**(9), 709–712 (2004)
22. Charbonnier, P., Blanc-Feraud, L., Aubert, G., Barlaud, M.: Deterministic edge-preserving regularization in computed imaging. IEEE Transactions on Image Processing **6**(2), 298–311 (1997)
23. Chartrand, R.: Exact reconstruction of sparse signals via nonconvex minimization. IEEE Signal Processing Letters **14**(10), 707–710 (2007)
24. Chartrand, R., Yin, W.: Iteratively reweighted algorithms for compressive sensing. In: Proceedings of IEEE Conference on Acoustics, Speech and Signal Processing, pp. 3869–3872 (2008)
25. Chen, S., Donoho, D.L., Saunders, M.: Atomic decomposition by basis pursuit. SIAM Review **43**(1), 129–159 (2001)
26. Chen, C., Huang, J., He, L.: Preconditioning for accelerated iteratively reweighted least squares in structured sparsity reconstruction. In: IEEE Conference on Computer Vision and Pattern Recognition (2014)
27. Cheng, B., Yang, J., Yan, S., Fu, Y., Huang, T.S.: Learning with ℓ_1-graph for image analysis. IEEE Transactions on Image Processing **4**, 858–866 (2010)
28. Chien, J.T., Wu, C.C.: Discriminant waveletfaces and nearest feature classifiers for face recognition. IEEE Transactions on Pattern Analysis and Machine Intelligence **24**(12), 1644–1649 (2002)
29. Combettes, P.L., Pesquet, J.C.: Proximal thresholding algorithm for minimization over orthonormal bases. SIAM Journal on Optimization **18**(4), 1531–1376 (2007)
30. Combettes, P.L., Wajs, V.R.: Signal recovery by proximal forward backward splitting. SIAM Journal on Multiscale Modeling & Simulation **4**(5), 1168–1200 (2005)
31. Cover, T., Thomas, J.: Elements of Information Theory, 2nd edition. New Jersey: John Wiley (2005)
32. Cover, T.M., Thomas, J.A.: Elements of information theory, 2nd edition. NewYork: John Wiley (2005)
33. Daubechies, I., Defrise, M., De Mol, C.: An iterative thresholding algorithm for linear inverse problems with a sparsity constraint. Communications in Pure and Applied Mathematics **57**, 1413–1457 (2006)
34. Daubechies, I., DeVore, R., Fornasier, M., Gunturk, C.: Iteratively re-weighted least squares minimization for sparse recovery. Communications on Pure and Applied Mathematics **63**(1), 1–38 (2010)
35. Davis, G., Mallat, S., Avellaneda, M.: Adaptive greedy approximations. Journal of Constructive Approximation **13**, 57–98 (1997)
36. Davis, J.V., Kulis, B., Jain, P., Sra, S., Dhillon, I.S.: Information-theoretic metric learning. In: International Conference on Machine Learning, pp. 209–216 (2007)
37. De la Torre, F., Black, M.: A framework for robust subspace learning. International Journal of Computer Vision **54**(1–3), 117–142 (2003)
38. Ding, C., Zhou, D., He, X., Zha, H.: R1-pca: rotational invariant L1-norm principal component analysis for robust subspace factorization. In: Proceedings of International Conference on Machine Learning

39. Donoho, D.L.: Compressed sensing. IEEE Transactions on Information Theory **52**(4), 1289–1306 (2006)
40. Donoho, D.L., Stodden, V.: Breakdown point of model selection when the number of variables exceeds the number of observations. In: Proceedings of the International Joint Conference on Neural Networks, pp. 16–21 (2006)
41. Donoho, D.L., Tanner, J.: Sparse nonnegative solutions of underdetermined linear equations by linear programming. In: Proceedings of the National Academy of Sciences, vol. 102, pp. 9446–9451 (2005)
42. Donoho, D.L., Tanner, J.: Observed universality of phase transitions in high-dimensional geometry, with implications for modern data analysis and signal processing. Philosophical Transactions of The Royal Society A **367**(1906), 4273–4293 (2009)
43. Donoho, D.L., Tsaig, Y.: Fast solution of l_1-norm minimization problems when the solution may be sparse. IEEE Transactions on Information Theory **54**(11), 4789–4812 (2008)
44. Donoho, D.L., Tsaig, Y., Drori, I., Starck, J.C.: Sparse solution of underdetermined systems of linear equations by stagewise orthogonal matching pursuit. IEEE Transactions on Information Theory **58**(2), 1094–1121 (2012)
45. Du, L., Li, X., Shen, Y.D.: Robust nonnegative matrix factorization via half-quadratic minimization. In: International Conference on Data Mining, pp. 201–210 (2012)
46. Elhamifar, E., Vidal, R.: Sparse subspace clustering: Algorithm, theory, and applications. Pattern Analysis and Machine Intelligence, IEEE Transactions on **35**(11), 2765–2781 (2013)
47. Fan, J., Li, R.: Statistical challenges with high dimensionality: Feature selection in knowledge discovery. In: the Madrid International Congress of Mathematicians, pp. 595–622
48. Feng, Y., Huang, X., Shi, L., Yang, Y., Suykens, J.A.K.: Learning with the maximum correntropy criterion induced losses for regression. Tech. rep., K.U.Leuven (Leuven, Belgium) (2013)
49. Fidler, S., Skocaj, D., Leonardis, A.: Combining reconstructive and discriminative subspace methods for robust classification and regression by subsampling. IEEE Transactions on Pattern Analysis and Machine Intelligence **28**(3), 337–350 (2006)
50. Figueiredo, M., Nowak, R., Wright, S.J.: Gradient projection for sparse reconstruction: application to compressed sensing and other inverse problems. IEEE Journal of Selected Topics in Signal Processing: Special Issue on Convex Optimization Methods for Signal Processing **1**(4), 586–597 (2007)
51. Forbes, A.: Classification-algorithm evaluation: Five performance measures based on confusion matrices. Journal of Clinical Monitoring and Computing **11**, 189–206 (1995)
52. Fornasier, M.: Theoretical foundations and numerical methods for sparse recovery. Radon Series on Computational and Applied Mathematics **9**, 1–121 (2010)
53. Gao, W., Cao, B., Shan, S., Chen, X., Zhou, D., Zhang, X., Zhao, D.: The cas-peal large-scale Chinese face database and baseline evaluations. IEEE Transactions on System Man, and Cybernetics (Part A) **38**(1), 149–161 (2008)
54. Geman, D., Reynolds, G.: Constrained restoration and recovery of discontinuities. IEEE Transactions on Pattern Analysis and Machine Intelligence **14**, 367–383 (1992)
55. Geman, D., Yang, C.: Nonlinear image recovery with half-quadratic regularization. IEEE Transactions on Image Processing **4**(7), 932–946 (1995)
56. Golub, G., Loan, C.V.: Matrix computations. 3rd edition. Johns Hopkins, Baltimore (1996)
57. Guyon, I., Elissee, A.: An introduction to variable and feature selection. Journal of Machine Learning Research **3**, 1157–1182 (2003)
58. He, R., Ao, M., Xiang, S., Li, S.: nearest feature line: a tangent approximation. In: Chinese Conference on Pattern Recognition (2008)
59. He, R., Hu, B.G., Yuan, X.: Robust discriminant analysis based on nonparametric maximum entropy. In: Asian Conference on Machine Learning (2009)
60. He, R., Hu, B.G., Yuan, X., Zheng, W.S.: Principal component analysis based on nonparametric maximum entropy. Neurocomputing **73**, 1840–1952 (2010)

61. He, R., Hu, B.G., Zheng, W.S., Guo, Y.Q.: Two-stage sparse representation for robust recognition on large-scale database. In: AAAI Conference on Artificial Intelligence, pp. 475–480 (2010)
62. He, R., Sun, Z., Tan, T., Zheng, W.S.: Recovery of corrupted low-rank matrices via half-quadratic based nonconvex minimization. In: IEEE Conference on Computer Vision and Pattern Recognition, pp. 2889–2896 (2011)
63. He, R., Tan, T., Wang, L.: Recovery of corrupted low-rank matrix by implicit regularizers. IEEE Transactions on Pattern Analysis and Machine Intelligence **36**(4), 770–783 (2014)
64. He, R., Tan, T., Wang, L., Zheng, W.S.: $\ell_{2,1}$ regularized correntropy for robust feature selection. In: Proceedings of IEEE Conference on Computer Vision and Pattern Recognition, pp. 2504–2511 (2012)
65. He, R., Zheng, W.S., Hu, B.G.: Maximum correntropy criterion for robust face recognition. IEEE Transactions on Pattern Analysis and Machine Intelligence **33**(8), 1561–1576 (2011)
66. He, R., Zheng, W.S., Hu, B.G., Kong, X.W.: Nonnegative sparse coding for discriminative semi-supervised learning. In: IEEE Conference on Computer Vision and Pattern Recognition, pp. 2849–2856 (2011)
67. He, R., Zheng, W.S., Hu, B.G., Kong, X.W.: A regularized correntropy framework for robust pattern recognition. Neural Computation **23**(8), 2074–2100 (2011)
68. He, R., Zheng, W.S., Hu, B.G., Kong, X.W.: Two-stage nonnegative sparse representation for large-scale face recognition. IEEE Transactions on Neural Network and Learning System **34**(1), 35–46 (2013)
69. He, R., Zheng, W.S., Tan, T., Sun, Z.: Half-quadratic based iterative minimization for robust sparse representation. IEEE Transactions on Pattern Analysis and Machine Intelligence **36**(2), 261–275 (2014)
70. He, X., Yan, S., Hu, Y., Niyogi, P., Zhang, H.J.: Face recognition using laplacianfaces. IEEE Transactions on Pattern Analysis and Machine Intelligence **27**(3), 328–340 (2005)
71. Hellier, P., Barillot, C., Memin, E., Perez, P.: An energy-based framework for dense 3D registration of volumetric brain images. In: Proceedings of IEEE Conference on Computer Vision and Pattern Recognition (2000)
72. Ho, J., Yang, M.H., Lim, J., Lee, K.C., Kriegman, D.: Clustering appearances of objects under varying illumination conditions. In: Proceedings of IEEE Conference on Computer Vision and Pattern Recognition, vol. 1, pp. 11–18 (2003)
73. Hotelling, H.: Analysis of a complex of statistical variables into principal components. Journal of Educational Psychology **24**, 417–441 (1933)
74. Hou, L., He, R.: Minimum entropy linear embedding based on gaussian mixture model. In: Asian Conference on Pattern Recognition, pp. 362–366 (2011)
75. Hu, B.G., He, R., Yuan, X.: Information-theoretic measures for objective evaluation of classifications. Acta Automatica Sinica **38**(7), 1169–1182 (2012)
76. Hu, B.G., Wang, Y.: Evaluation criteria based on mutual information for classifications including rejected class. Acta Automatica Sinica **34**, 1396–1403 (2008)
77. Huber, P.: Robust statistics. Wiley (1981)
78. Hyvarinen, A.: Fast and robust fixed-point algorithms for independent component analysis. IEEE Transactions on Neural Networks **10**, 626–634 (1999)
79. Hyvärinen, A.: Survey on independent component analysis. Neural Computing Surveys **2**, 94–128 (1999)
80. Idier, J.: Convex half-quadratic criteria and interacting auxiliary variables for image restoration. IEEE Transactions on Image Processing **10**(7), 1001–1009 (2001)
81. Jenssen, R., D.Erdogmus, Principe, J., Eltoft, T.: Information theoretic angle-based spectral clustering: a theoretical analysis and an algorithm. In: International joint conference on neural networks, pp. 4904–4911 (2006)
82. Jenssen, R., Eltoft, T., Girolami, M., Erdogmus, D.: Kernel maximum entropy data transformation and an enhanced spectral clustering algorithm. In: Neural Information Processing Systems NIPS (2006)

83. Jeonga, K.H., Liu, W.F., Han, S., Hasanbelliu, E., Principe, J.C.: The correntropy mace filter. Pattern Recognition **42**(5), 871–885 (2009)
84. Ji, Y., Lin, T., Zha, H.: Mahalanobis distance based non-negative sparse representation for face recognition. In: Proceedings of International Conference on Machine Learning and Applications, pp. 41–46 (2009)
85. Jia, H., Martinez, A.M.: Face recognition with occlusions in the training and testing sets. In: IEEE International Conference on Automatic Face & Gesture Recognition (2008)
86. Jia, H., Martinez, A.M.: Support vector machines in face recognition with occlusions. In: Proceedings of IEEE Conference on Computer Vision and Pattern Recognition, pp. 136–141 (2009)
87. Kapur, J.: Measures of information and their applications. John Wiley, New York (1994)
88. Laaksonen, J.: Local subspace classifier. In: International Conference on Artificial Neural Networks (1997)
89. Lee, H., Battle, A., Raina, R., Ng, A.Y.: Efficient sparse coding algorithms. In: Proceedings of Neural Information Processing Systems, vol. 19, pp. 801–808 (2006)
90. Lei, Z., Chu, R., He, R., Liao, S., Li, S.Z.: Face recognition by discriminant analysis with Gabor tensor representation. In: Advances in Biometrics (2010)
91. Leonardis, A., Bischof, H.: Robust recognition using eigenimages. Computer Vision and Image Understanding **78**(1), 99–118 (2000)
92. Li, M., Chen, X., Li, X., Ma, B., Vitanyi, M.: The similarity metric. IEEE Transactions Information Theory **50**, 3250–3264 (2004)
93. Li, S.Z.: Face recognition based on nearest linear combinations. In: Proceedings of IEEE Conference on Computer Vision and Pattern Recognition, pp. 839–844 (1998)
94. Li, S.Z., Lu, J.: Face recognition using the nearest feature line method. IEEE Transactions Neural Network **10**(2), 439–443 (1999)
95. Li, W., Swetits, J.J.: The linear ℓ_1 estimator and the Huber m-estimator. SIAM Journal on Optimization **8**(2), 457–475 (1998)
96. Li, X.X., Dai, D.Q., Zhang, X.F., Ren, C.X.: Structured sparse error coding for face recognition with occlusion. IEEE Transactions on Image Processing **22**(5), 1889–1900 (2013)
97. Lin, D.: An information-theoretic definition of similarity. In: International Conference on Machine Learning, pp. 296–304 (1998)
98. Liu, R., Li, S.Z., Yuan, X., He, R.: Online determination of track loss using template inverse matching. In: International Workshop on Visual Surveillance-VS (2008)
99. Liu, W.F., Pokharel, P.P., Principe, J.C.: Correntropy: Properties and applications in non-gaussian signal processing. IEEE Transactions on Signal Processing **55**(11), 5286–5298 (2007)
100. Luenberger, D.: Optimization by vector space methods. Wiley (1969)
101. Mairal, J., Elad, M., Sapiro, G.: Sparse representation for color image restoration. IEEE Transactions on Image Processing **17**(1), 53–69 (2008)
102. Mairal, J., Sapiro, G., Elad, M.: Learning multiscale sparse representations for image and video restoration. SIAM Multiscale Modeling & Simulation **7**(1), 214–241 (2008)
103. Martinez, A.M., Benavente, R.: The AR face database. Tech. rep., Computer Vision Center (1998)
104. Mathar, R., Schmeink, A.: Saddle-point properties and nash equilibria for channel games. EURASIP Journal on Advances in Signal Processing (2009)
105. Mazeta, V., Carteretb, C., Briea, D., Idierc, J., Humbert, B.: Background removal from spectra by designing and minimising a non-quadratic cost function. Chemometrics and Intelligent Laboratory Systems **76**(2), 121–133 (2005)
106. Meer, P., Stewart, C., Tyler, D.: Robust computer vision: An interdisciplinary challenge, guest editorial. Computer Vision and Image Understanding **78**, 1–7 (2000)
107. Morejon, R.A., Principe, J.C.: Advanced search algorithms for information-theoretic learning with kernel-based estimators. IEEE Transactions on Neural Networks **15**(4), 874–884 (2004)
108. Moulin, P., O'Sullivan, J.A.: Information-theoretic analysis of information hiding. IEEE Transactions on Information Theory **49**(3), 563–593 (2003)

109. Naseem, I., Togneri, R., Bennamoun, M.: Linear regression for face recognition. IEEE Transactions on Pattern Analysis and Machine Intelligence **32**(11), 2106–2112 (2010)
110. Nenadic, Z.: Information discriminant analysis: feature extraction with an information-theoretic objective. IEEE Transactions on Pattern Analysis and Machine Intelligence **29**(8), 1394–1407 (2007)
111. Newman, D., Hettich, S., Blake, C., Merz, C.: Uci repository of machine learning databases. http://www.ics.uci.edu/mlearn/MLRepository.html (1998)
112. Nikolova, M., NG, M.K.: Analysis of half-quadratic minimization methods for signal and image recovery. SIAM Journal on Scientific Computing **27**(3), 937–966 (2005)
113. Nishii, R., Tanaka, S.: Accuracy and inaccuracy assessments in land-cover classification. IEEE Transactions Geoscience and Remote Sensing **37**, 491–498 (1999)
114. Niu, G., Dai, B., Yamada, M., Sugiyama, M.: Information-theoretic semi-supervised metric learning via entropy regularization. In: International Conference on Machine Learning (2012)
115. Niu, G., Jitkrittum, W., Dai, B., Hachiya, H., Sugiyama, M.: Squared-loss mutual information regularization: A novel information-theoretic approach to semi-supervised learning. In: International Conference on Machine Learning (2013)
116. Nowak, R., Figueiredo, M.: Fast wavelet-based image deconvolution using the EM algorithm. In: Proceedings of Asilomar Conference on Signals, Systems, and Computers, vol. 1, pp. 371–375 (2001)
117. Parzen, E.: On the estimation of probability density function and the mode. The Annals of Mathematical Statistics **33**, 1065–1076 (1962)
118. Patel, V.M., Chellappa, R.: Sparse Representations and Compressive Sensing for Imaging and Vision. SpringerBriefs in Electrical and Computer Engineering (2013)
119. Pearson, K.: On lines and planes of closest fit to systems of points in space. The London, Edinburgh and Dublin Philosophical Magazine and Journal of Science, Sixth Series **2**, 559–572 (1901)
120. Peng, H., Long, F., Ding, C.: Feature selection based on mutual information: criteria of max-dependency, max-relevance, and min-redundancy. IEEE Transactions on Pattern Analysis and Machine Intelligence **27**(8), 1226–1238 (2005)
121. Plumbley, M.: Recovery of sparse representations by polytope faces pursuit. In: Proceedings of International Conference on Independent Component Analysis and Blind Source Separation, pp. 206–213 (2006)
122. Pokharel, P.P., Liu, W., Principe, J.C.: A low complexity robust detector in impulsive noise. Signal Processing **89**(10), 1902–1909 (2009)
123. Portugal, L.F., Judice, J.J., Vicente, L.N.: A comparison of block pivoting and interior-point algorithms for linear least squares problems with nonnegative variables. Mathematics of Computation **63**(208), 625–643 (1994)
124. Principe, J., Xu, D., Zhao, Q., Fisher, J.: Learning from examples with information-theoretic criteria. Journal of VLSI Signal Processing **26**, 61–77 (2000)
125. Principe, J.C.: Information Theoretic Learning: Renyi's Entropy and Kernel Perspectives. Springer (2010)
126. Principe, J.C., Xu, D., Fisher, J.W.: Information-theoretic learning. In: S. Haykin, editor, Unsupervised Adaptive Filtering, Volume 1: Blind-Source Separation. Wiley (2000)
127. P.Viola, N.Schraudolph, T.Sejnowski: Empirical entropy manipulation for real-world problems. In: Proceedings of Neural Information Processing Systems, pp. 851–857 (1995)
128. Rao, S., Liu, W., Principe, J.C., de Medeiros Martins, A.: Information theoretic mean shift algorithm. In: Machine Learning for Signal Processing (2006)
129. Renyi, A.: On measures of entropy and information. Selected Papers of Alfred Renyi **2**, 565–580 (1976)
130. Reshef, D.N., Reshef, Y.A., Finucane, H.K., Grossman, S.R., McVean, G., Turnbaugh, P.J., Lander, E.S., Mitzenmacher, M. Sabeti, P.C.: Detecting novel associations in large data sets. Science **334**, 1518–1524 (2011)
131. Rockfellar, R.: Convex analysis. Princeton Press (1970)

132. Roullot, E., Herment, A., Bloch, I., de Cesare, A., Nikolova, M., Mousseaux, E.: Modeling anisotropic undersampling of magnetic resonance angiographies and reconstruction of a high-resolution isotropic volume using half-quadratic regularization techniques. Signal Processing **84**(4), 743–762 (2004)
133. Rousseeuw, P.J.: Least median of squares regression. Journal of the American Statistical Association **79**(388), 871–880 (1984)
134. Roweis, S.: EM algorithms for PCA and SPCA. In: Neural Information Processing Systems (NIPS), pp. 626–632 (1997)
135. Santamaria, I., Pokharel, P.P., Principe, J.C.: Generalized correlation function: Definition, properties, and application to blind equalization. IEEE Transactions on Signal Processing **54**(6), 2187–2197 (2006)
136. Seth, S., Principe, J.C.: Compressed signal reconstruction using the correntropy induced metric. In: Proceedings of IEEE Conference on Acoustics, Speech and Signal Processing, pp. 3845–3848 (2008)
137. Shannon, C.: A mathematical theory of communication. Bell System Technical Journal **27**, 623–653 (1948)
138. Sharma, A., Paliwal, K.: Fast principal component analysis using fixed-point algorithm. Pattern Recognition Letters **28**, 1151–1155 (2007)
139. Shi, Q., Eriksson, A., van den Hengel, A., Shen, C.: Face recognition really a compressive sensing problem. In: Proceedings of IEEE Conference on Computer Vision and Pattern Recognition, pp. 553–560 (2011)
140. Shi, Y., Sha, F.: Information-theoretical learning of discriminative clusters for unsupervised domain adaptation. In: International Conference on Machine Learning (2012)
141. Siegel, A.F.: Robust regression using repeated medians. Biometrika **69**(1), 242–244 (1982)
142. Sun, X.: Matrix Perturbation Analysis. Chinese Science Press (2001)
143. Takhar, D., Laska, J., Wakin, M., Duarte, M., Baron, D., Sarvotham, S., Kelly, K., , Baraniuk, R.: A new compressive imaging camera architecture using optical-domain compression. In: Proceedings of Computational Imaging IV at SPIE Electronic Imaging, pp. 43–52 (2006)
144. Tao, D., Li, X., Wu, X., Maybank, S.: Tensor rank one discriminant analysis - a convergent method for discriminative multilinear subspace selection. Neurocomputing **71**, 1866–1882 (2008)
145. Torkkola, K.: Feature extraction by nonparametric mutual information maximization. Journal of Machine Learning Research **3**, 1415–1438 (2003)
146. Vapnik, V.: The Nature of Statistical Learning Theory. New York: Springer-Verlag (1995)
147. Vincent, P., Bengio, Y.: K-local hyperplane and convex distance nearest neighbor algorithms. In: Advances in Neural Information Processing Systems, vol. 14, pp. 985–992 (2001)
148. Vinh, N.X., Epps, J., Bailey, J.: Information theoretic measures for clusterings comparison: Variants, properties, normalization and correction for chance. Journal of Machine Learning Research **11**, 2837–2854 (2010)
149. Vo, N., Moran, B., Challa, S.: Nonnegative-least-square classifier for face recognition. In: Proceedings of International Symposium on Neural Networks:Advances in Neural Networks, pp. 449–456 (2009)
150. Wakin, M., Laska, J., Duarte, M., Baron, D., Sarvotham, S., Takhar, D., Kelly, K., Baraniuk, R.: An architecture for compressive image. In: Proceedings of International Conference on Image Processing, pp. 1273–1276 (2006)
151. Wang, S., Liu, D., Zhang, Z: Nonconvex Relaxation approaches to robust matrix recovery. In: International Joint Conferences on Artificial Intelligence (2013)
152. Weiszfeld, E.: Sur le point pour lequel la somme des distances de n points donnes est minimum. Mathematical Journal **43**, 355–386 (1937)
153. Wright, J., Ma, Y.: Dense error correction via ℓ_1-minimization. IEEE Transactions on Information Theory **56**(7), 3540–3560 (2010)
154. Wright, J., Ma, Y., Mairal, J., Sapiro, G., Huang, T.S., Yan, S.: Sparse representation for computer vision and pattern recognition. Proceedings of IEEE **98**(6), 1031–1044 (2010)

155. Wright, J., Yang, A.Y., Ganesh, A., Sastry, S.S., Ma, Y.: Robust face recognition via sparse representation. IEEE Transactions on Pattern Analysis and Machine Intelligence **31**(2), 210–227 (2009)
156. Wright, S., Nowak, R., Figueiredo, M.: Sparse reconstruction by separable approximation. In: Proceedings of IEEE Conference on Acoustics, Speech and Signal Processing (2008)
157. Xing, E.P., Ng, A.Y., Jordan, M.I., Russell, S.: Distance metric learning with application to clustering with side-information. In: Proceedings of Advances in Neural Information Processing Systems, vol. 15, pp. 505–512 (2002)
158. Xu, D.: Energy, entropy and information potential for neural computation. Ph.D. thesis, University of Florida (1999)
159. Yan, H., Yuan, X., Yan, S., Yang, J.: Correntropy based feature selection using binary projection. Pattern Recognition **44**, 2834–2842 (2011)
160. Yan, S., Xu, D., Zhang, B., Zhang, H., Yang, Q., Lin, S.: Graph embedding and extensions: a general framework for dimensionality reduction. IEEE Transactions on Pattern Analysis and Machine Intelligence **29**(1), 40–51 (2007)
161. Yang, A.Y., Sastry, S.S., Ganesh, A., Ma, Y.: Fast ℓ_1-minimization algorithms and an application in robust face recognition: A review. In: Proceedings of International Conference on Image Processing (2010)
162. Yang, M., Zhang, L., Yang, J., Zhang, D.: Robust sparse coding for face recognition. In: Proceedings of IEEE Conference on Computer Vision and Pattern Recognition, pp. 625–632 (2011)
163. Yang, S., Zha, H., Zhou, S., Hu, B.G.: Variational graph embedding for globally and locally consistent feature extraction. In: Europe Conference on Machine Learning (ECML), pp. 538–553 (2009)
164. Yin, W., Osher, S., Goldfarb, D., Darbon, J.: Bregman iterative algorithms for ℓ_1-minimization with applications to compressed sensing. SIAM Journal on Imaging Sciences **1**(1), 143–168 (2008)
165. Yuan, X.T., Hu, B.G.: Robust feature extraction via information theoretic learning. In: Proceedings of International Conference on Machine Learning, pp. 1193–1200 (2009)
166. Yuan, X.T., Li, S.: Half quadratic analysis for mean shift: with extension to a sequential data mode-seeking method. In: IEEE International Conference on Computer Vision (2007)
167. Zhang, L., Yang, M., Feng, X.: Sparse representation or collaborative representation: Which helps face recognition? In: Proceedings of IEEE International Conference on Computer Vision (2011)
168. Zhang, T.: Multi-stage convex relaxation for learning with sparse regularization. In: Proceedings of Neural Information Processing Systems, pp. 16–21 (2008)
169. Zhang, T.H., Tao, D.C., Li, X.L., Yang, J.: Patch alignment for dimensionality reduction. IEEE Trans. Knowl. Data Eng. **21**(9), 1299–1313 (2009)
170. Zhang, Y., Sun, Z., He, R., Tan, T.: Robust low-rank representation via correntropy. In: Asian Conference on Pattern Recognition (2013)
171. Zhang, Y., Sun, Z., He, R., Tan, T.: Robust subspace clustering via half-quadratic minimization. In: International Conference on Computer Vision (2013)
172. Zhang, Z.: Parameter estimation techniques: A tutorial with application to conic fitting. Image and Vision Computing **15**(1), 59–76 (1997)
173. Zou, H.: The adaptive lasso and its oracle properties. Journal of the American Statistical Association **101**(476), 1418–1429 (2006)